PROPAGANDA POSTCARDS
of World War II

By Ron Menchine

Best wishes,
Ron Menchine

krause publications

700 East State Street • Iola, WI 54990-0001
715/445-2214 • FAX: 715/445-4087   www.krause.com

Please call or write for our free catalog of publications. Our toll-free number to place an order
or obtain a free catalog is 800-258-0929 or please use our regular business
telephone 715-445-2214 for editorial comment and further information.

Library of Congress Catalog Number: 99-67647

ISBN: 1-58221-024-1

Printed in the United States of America

Dedication

I dedicate this book to my late father, Judge W. Albert Menchine, who served with distinction in the Counter Intelligence Corps during World War II in Australia, New Guinea, the Philippines, and Korea and whose fascinating letters home first stimulated my interest in World War II history.

Special Thanks

To Leon Rowe, friend and co-author on a future book, who diligently computerized my text and offered valuable suggestions every step of the way.

And to Dr. Greg Bradsher, Director of the Holocaust Era Assets Records Project and former Assistant Manager of Modern Military and Intelligence Records at the National Archives and Records Administration, whose encouragement and advice helped make this project a reality and who graciously wrote the foreword.

Acknowledgments

Major Mel Bailey, United States Air Force Retired, who spent three years with the Air Force in Japan and, with help from Japanese friends, translated the Japanese cards in this book.

J. Boekhorst, Counselor for Press and Cultural Affairs at the Royal Netherlands Embassy in Washington, D.C., who supplied information on Dutch artists Nico Broekman and Ton Smits.

Donald R. Brown, Executive Director for the Institute of American Deltiology, for his background information on many American publishers.

Paul Dickson and the late James Thorpe III, who first suggested I write this book.

Ken Fleck and Don Preziosi, fellow World War II propaganda postcard collectors who provided information from their own outstanding collections.

Helma Frantz, wife of postcard collector and dealer Leo Frantz, who translated the German cards.

Gordon Gilkey, Curator Emeritus of the Portland Art Museum in Oregon, who, during World War II headed the Joint Chiefs of Staff Study of Nazi Psychological Warfare and who supplied useful information on Nazi propaganda.

Tonie and Valmai Holt, longtime British friends and World War II historians, authors, and military tour guides, who shared valuable information on propaganda postcards.

Henry Patrick, longtime friend, who provided research material for the book.

Gilbert Pittman and Roberta Greiner, whose checklist of World War II military comics proved invaluable.

Michail A. Shurgalin, Press Counselor at the Russian Embassy in Washington, D.C., who not only translated the captions on the Russian postcards but taught me much about Russian World War II propaganda operations as well as Russian history.

John Taylor, longtime archivist at the National Archives in Washington, D.C., who pointed me in the right direction at the beginning of this project nearly ten years ago.

Inka Vostrezova, First Secretary, Cultural Section, Embassy of the Czech and Slovak Federal Republic, for providing background information on the Czech cards.

Foreword

During World War II the war was fought on many fronts. There were the military and intelligence fronts, the financial and economic fronts, the diplomatic front, the home front, and the propaganda front. The propaganda efforts during the war influenced all of the other fronts. Generally, propaganda was used for two purposes. One was to uphold the valor and values, and the rightness of the cause, of a particular country. The other was to despise their opponents; to demonize them, to label them as warmongers and criminals.

When we think of United States World War II propaganda, what usually comes to mind are the movies and newsreels. Actually, propaganda by the warring parties, including the United States, as well as propaganda by the neutral nations, was quite extensive, ranging to all forms of communication. Included were leaflet-dropping operations, pamphlets and forged pamphlets, posters, radio and shortwave broadcasts, newspapers, speeches, songs, political cartoons, and even whispering campaigns.

I am somewhat knowledgeable about American propaganda as I have made extensive use of the records of the Office of War Information and the Office of Strategic Services (OSS), the Office of Inter American Affairs and the War Department, and records of other government agencies at the National Archives. Documented in those records are countless examples of propaganda efforts by the United States as well as information about enemy propaganda and efforts to counteract such efforts. Interestingly enough in those records, to the best of my knowledge there is no information about postcards being used for propaganda purposes. There is information about philatelic areas of propaganda, such as the OSS-produced German postage stamps showing Hitler's face, half of which was a skull, indicating the fate that awaited him and his followers.

About nine years ago I became interested in postcards and it was not too much later that I came across a commercially-produced postcard depicting soldiers kicking Hitler and another showing Hitler, Mussolini, and Tojo being flushed down a toilet. During the succeeding years I ran across many such postcards. I found them interesting and instructive, giving a pictorial view, often in a humorous manner, of American hatred for Hitler, Mussolini, and Tojo, as well as Japanese soldiers. I ran across few postcards depicting similar negativity about Italian and German soldiers. But of course I knew from my historical studies that the Japanese were viewed, because of racial stereotypes, quite differently than the people of other Axis countries. The Japanese, or "Japs" as they were most often identified, were frequently described by Americans as treacherous, sly, and cruel.

I became intrigued with these American propaganda postcards and wanted to learn more about them. Unfortunately, I could not find much literature on the subject. Thus I was very pleased when my friend Ron Menchine told me he was writing a book on the subject. Being familiar with Ron's book about baseball postcards, I knew that what he would produce would be valuable, not only to collectors but undoubtedly to those interested in World War II propaganda. What was even more pleasing to me was that his book would include propaganda postcards produced in many of the warring and neutral nations. When he first informed me of this fact, I told him I had never seen a non-American World War II propaganda postcard. In short order, Ron showed me several. I was suitably impressed and my immediate thought was, "Wow, these non-American propaganda postcards will enhance our knowledge of how non-American countries viewed their enemies."

So, now almost two years from the time we first talked about his propaganda postcard book, I have followed Ron's efforts at expanding his collection of propaganda postcards and increasing his subject matter expertise. Now the book is completed. Ron has produced a real contribution to our understanding of World War II propaganda and has added a significant contribution to our knowledge of postcards and their use as propaganda.

Greg Bradsher
Silver Spring, Maryland

Table of Contents

Preview

Propaganda postcards did not originate with World War II or World War I for that matter. Postcards were used as a propaganda tool as early as the Boer War in South Africa before the turn of the century. The purpose of any propaganda postcard is quite simple - to poke fun at or demonize the enemy while glorifying your own side. I begin this book by showing a few propaganda postcards from World War I because many of the same techniques were used 21 years later when World War II broke out.

It is widely acknowledged that Great Britain produced the most effective propaganda postcards. In fact, German Chancellor Adolph Hitler wrote, "What we failed to do in propaganda (during World War I) was done by the enemy with great skill and ingenious deliberation." Therefore, he made every effort to make German World War II propaganda second to none and with his skilled propaganda minister, Joseph Goebbels, succeeded in this effort.

But no matter how effective your propaganda is, there is no substitute for victories on the battlefield. German propaganda was highly effective early in the war, but once the Allies began winning, it lost much of its effectiveness. However, the theme reiterated late in the war was that Russians were barbarians and would commit unspeakable crimes if they ever won the war. Fear of the Russian army, with some justification, was exploited adroitly by Goebbels and unquestionably had the Germans fighting hard right up to the end. Goebbels called this form of propaganda "strength through fear."

Surprisingly, Germany's World War II postcard propaganda almost exclusively glorified Hitler, his military, and the German people without demeaning the enemy. His Axis partner Italy, on the other hand, did just the opposite. Although they had their share of patriotic postcard themes, many were devoted to demonizing the enemy and its leaders. Japan's propaganda was more like Germany's. Even though their cards would occasionally show a Japanese soldier trampling on an American or British flag, most glorified their military and depicted their soldiers as extremely friendly toward the people they conquered.

Most of the Allied propaganda postcards of World War II originated in the United States. Even though the war had been going on for over two years when Japan attacked Pearl Harbor, the United States began producing anti-Axis cards almost immediately and quickly surpassed all the other Allied nations. Germany made such quick work of its enemies that after June 1940, Great Britain stood alone against the Nazi oppressors. The conquered nations obviously had no opportunity to produce anti-Axis postcards. Next to the United States, Great Britain produced the most and, as in World War I, they were quite good. In fact, many of the same British artists worked in both wars.

This book is divided into four sections: cards exclusive to the United States; cards from its Allied partners; cards of the Axis powers; and cards from neutral nations. Altogether, propaganda postcards from 25 different nations are represented and you will see how the style of propaganda differed from one to another. Some are crude and scatological, others are meticulous and superbly drawn, but all are fascinating. I proudly present *Propaganda Postcards of World War II.*

Ron Menchine

A Few World War I Propaganda Postcards

French, by L. Miral, 1915.

Glancing furtively over his shoulder, the Kaiser finds the grim reaper in hot pursuit in this powerful graphic by French artist L. Miral. Part of a rare eight-card set vividly hand-colored by the artist, on this card Miral projects a sad end for Kaiser Wilhelm. Ironically, the Kaiser not only survived the war, he lived to see a corporal from his own army, Adolph Hitler, on the verge of achieving a European conquest that he never could. Exiled to Holland in 1918, the Kaiser lived comfortably and quietly. When Germany conquered Paris on June 14, 1940, the Kaiser sent a congratulatory telegram to Hitler on his "mighty victory granted by God." The Kaiser died of natural causes, content in his belief that Germany ruled the world.

French, by Igor, published by P & J Gallais.

The French artist Igor, using a devastating twist to the "God Is With Us" theme, shows the Kaiser dragging Jesus Christ shackled to the tail of the horse he is riding through a cross-laden cemetery. To further the humiliation, the Kaiser is wielding a five-tailed whip. Published by P & J Gallais of Paris, this series featured many famous French artists such as Igor, Fumy, and Zislin and depicted the horrific effects of war with captions in both English and French.

Right: Political cartoonist Louis Raemakers was one of the most prolific World War I propaganda artists. Working for the Dutch newspaper, *De Telegraaf* of Amsterdam, Raemakers produced a series of postcards and booklets of postcards (from which the buyer tore out cards as needed) audaciously titled "Drawings of a Neutral," which were sold for the benefit of French and British wounded. Anything but neutral, nearly all of Raemakers' drawings were virulently anti-German and took on such themes as the German passion for order and organization even when committing atrocities. In one of his postcards, German troops are getting ready to slaughter civilians and the caption reads, "Everything in good order, women to the left."

This example shows the Kaiser and Crown Prince worriedly viewing an hourglass with blood from the bodies of German soldiers representing the sands of time. Poignantly titled "Will They Last?" the subtitle states, "The grave question with Germany has long been one of manpower." Over a million German soldiers were killed in four years of war. Another Raemakers postcard has a German soldier in a trench stretching for good news to write home about. He writes, "We gained a good bit, our Cemeteries stretch as far as the sea already."

John Lafflin, in his *World War I in Postcards*, suggests that Raemaekers' postcards were for the more discerning

© 1019

"WILL THEY LAST?"
The grave question with Germany has long been one of man power.

United States version, by Louis Raemakers, published by Brown Robertson Co.

buyers as "they did not sell in large numbers." But the images themselves - the cartoons - had an enormous impact, especially those powerful works on the German invasion of Belgium. To a large degree, Raemaekers' most poignant propaganda was, by his own admission, based on the Bryce Report, the British report on German atrocities in Belgium, replete with mass rapes, children spitted on bayonets, and hostage murders. Years later, Great Britain candidly admitted many of the "facts" in the Bryce Report were false.

IT NEVER RAINS BUT IT POURS

British, by Alfred Leete, published by Lawrence and Jellicoe.

Left: British artist Alfred Leete is most famous for his World War I recruiting poster, "Your King and Country Need You." He was also a gifted caricaturist as this design showing artillery shells of 11 countries raining down on the Kaiser would indicate. This postcard was published by Lawrence and Jellicoe of London prior to the entry of the United States into the war on April 6, 1917. Leete contributed to such British magazines as *The Passing Show* and was president of the London Sketch Club in 1925.

British, by Reg Carter, published by British Art Co.

Reg Carter was 28 years old when World War I broke out in 1914 and already a successful comic postcard artist. He was born and spent most of his 64 years in Southwold, Suffolk. A member of the North British Academy, his art was featured in such magazines as *The Sketch* and *The Tattler*. Uncle Sam (still neutral) is disdainfully looking at the names Louvain and Rheims, both severely damaged by German artillery, while the Kaiser tries to get his attention. British propaganda, much superior to that of the Germans in World War I, blamed them for many atrocities that did not actually occur and proved an effective tool in helping persuade the United States to join the Allies. This vast propaganda disparity did not go unnoticed by Adolph Hitler, who vowed things would be different if there was a "next war" which began only 21 years after World War I ended. Much of Hitler's success was achieved by propaganda brilliance under the direction of Dr. Joseph Goebbels.

British, by F.G. Lewin, published by E. Mack, Hampstead, London.

F.G. Lewin's tactic of depicting the Kaiser as a "Mad Dog" is one used by all sides in both World Wars. Denigrating the opposing leaders by portraying them as animals proved successful in World War I and II and was used as a propaganda tool as recently as the Desert Storm campaign against Saddam Hussein. If Lewin did not originate the Mad Dog theme, he was certainly among the first to use it. Eighty years later, it's still effective.

Belgium, published by MaCampagne, Brussels.

This powerful Belgian card shows a smiling Kaiser Wilhelm of Germany and Emperor Franz Joseph of Austria/Hungary standing in the foreground of a sea of corpses and cemetery crosses under the slogan "Gott Ist Mit Uns" (God Is With Us). The message epitomizes the madness of a belief prevalent since the Crusades. Regardless of how worthy or unworthy a particular nation's cause, they invariably invoke the Almighty's beneficence as exclusively theirs. Approximately 300,000 Belgian troops lost their lives in the Great War, nearly three times the number of casualties suffered by the United States. Seven million Allied troops were killed in action while Germany, Austria/Hungary, Turkey, and Bulgaria lost three million lives. (Apparently God was looking the other way, at least part of the time.)

United States, published by the Young Men's Christian Association (YMCA), mailed July 31, 1918.

Political cartoonists have frequently used baseball as a metaphor. The German assertion that they were at war to spread "kultur" was widely ridiculed and turned into grist for the propaganda machine. The Kaiser, with a bloody sword in one hand, has just pitched "kultur" to Uncle Sam, who has threatened to knock the cover off the ball.

11

About Pricing

Pricing any collectible is hardly an exact science. Many factors enter into the picture including condition, rarity, desirability, and in the case of postcards, aesthetic appeal. Perhaps the most important determinate is what the dealer originally paid for the item. Dealers will normally double the original price, which enables them to allow a discount and still make a profit. Because dealers pay different prices for the same item, retail prices will often vary considerably.

During the past 25 years, my quest for propaganda postcards from World War II has taken me to shows throughout the United States as well as England and France. In addition, I have purchased and traded these items with collectors throughout the world.

Generally, a good rule of thumb to follow is that the more common World War II propaganda postcards fall into the $10 to $15 price range. Those more desirable will fetch between $15 and $25. When the card is well above average, the price will fluctuate between $25 and $50. The exceptional cards such as the Califano, Szyk, and Berdanier artist-signed United States cards pictured in the book will command a minimum of $50 and at auction could bring considerably more. These prices are based on the cards being in "mint" condition, meaning that they aren't creased, bent, stained, or torn. They may be postally used and still be considered mint. Throughout the book, I've noted which cards fall

This relatively common card by Walter Wellman is valued at $10 to $25.

An outstanding card by an unknown artist, this piece is valued at $25 to $50.

This card by Arthur Szyk was published by Esquire *magazine in 1942. It is valued at $50 and up.*

into the $25 to $50 range and which are so exceptional that they would fetch at least $50. The balance of the cards range from $10 to $25.

Another interesting variable is where the card is sold. Prices vary from one country to the other, although the gap is rapidly closing. Generally, a British card will sell for less in the United States than in the United Kingdom and vice versa. Of all the foreign cards produced during World War II, Italian cards featuring exceptional art, particularly those done by Gino Boccasile, rank among the best and highest priced. Since the tearing down of the "Iron Curtain," Russian cards are beginning to circulate, and although often on poor quality stock, they rank among the finest, especially those created by the Kukryniksy consortium. You will be able to see and admire all of the above mentioned cards in this book.

Propaganda Postcards of World War II - United States

As war clouds gathered in the 1930s, American anti-war groups demanded drastic reduction in United States armament budgets by producing postcards and posters detailing how expensive war would be. This graphically explicit postcard produced by World Peace Posters, Inc., 31 Union Square in New York City, depicts the cost of $1,300 for a single bomb. It is one of seven equally powerful designs produced in both poster and postcard form. The combination of pacifistic longings and pro-Hitler sentiment (primarily but by no means exclusively among Americans of German descent) made military preparation politically difficult - that is until December 8, 1941. The distinctively Art Deco style of this design was considered futuristic in the 1930s.

United States, published by World Peace Posters, New York, value $25-$50.

There's a sad and fascinating story behind this Michael Califano anti-Nazi postcard produced in 1934 showing Hitler ordering Albert Einstein out of Germany. Proceeds from the sale of these postcards went to Jewish refugees who were fleeing the Nazi leader. Califano himself was a refugee from Italy who left his homeland in 1922 to seek a better life in America. Born in Naples in 1889, he enrolled in the city's Fine Arts Academy. His work was discovered by Italy's King Vittorio Emanuelle, who sent him to the Austrian front during World War I to capture battle scenes on canvas. Unfortunately, the roar of constant bombardment made Califano deaf.

After the war he became one of three painters in the Royal Court but longed for the fame and fortune he hoped to find in America. His deafness, combined with the fact that the Italian quota of immigrants had already been reached, almost prevented him from entering the United States at Ellis Island. Deaf and unable to speak English, to prove his artistic skills Califano found a scrap of wood on which he painted a young Dutch girl, thus charming immigration officials and leading to his admittance. His wife and three children soon followed. Despite his handicap, his enormous skill as a portrait painter and landscape artist enabled him to establish an excellent reputation. Califano painted many celebrities including Charles Lindbergh and movie heartthrob Rudolph Valentino. His portrait of Valentino as a toreador brought $12,000, an enormous sum in the 1920s.

In 1934, outraged over Hitler's treatment of Jews, Califano produced "The Ignominy of the Twentieth Century," a life-size painting from which this postcard was derived. The painting infuriated Nazi sympathizers in the United States and changed the artist's life forever. On May 16, 1935, as Califano was working in his Manhattan studio preparing for a major show the next day, three men broke in, tied the artist up, beat him senseless, and destroyed 30 canvasses with knives. Some of the destroyed paintings belonged to other artists and without vandalism insurance, Califano spent much of the remainder of his life paying off the debt. The three assailants were never caught.

He continued to work but literally became a recluse in his son's home in Lattingtown, New York. He died in 1979 at the age of 90, a broken and bitter man. It's ironic that a painting designed to help people in need in the end brought Michael Califano nothing but grief.

United States, by Michael Califano, published by Michael Califano, 1934, value $50 and up.

This gruesome postcard showing Hitler as an enraged madman destroying civilization is American, and surprisingly, was published in 1940, nearly two years before the United States entered the war. The artist and publisher are unknown, but they depict the horrific aspects of war exceptionally well. Note Hitler is wearing a skull mask portraying death, while he torches homes, causing the terrified population to flee in panic. Unfortunately, this scene was repeated many times before the war finally ended in 1945. The legend on the back of the card is nearly as interesting as the front:

Barbarism Against Civilization!
Paganism Against Christianity!
1870: France Devastated, Population Robbed and Murdered.
1914: France and Belgium Devastated, Population Robbed and Murdered.

United States, 1940, value $25-$50.

1939: Czechoslovakia and Poland Devastated, Population Robbed and Murdered.
1940: Denmark, Norway, Holland, Belgium, Luxemburg,(sic) France Devastated, Population Robbed and Murdered.
WHO IS NEXT?
Shall We Allow Destruction and World Conquest by Barbarism?
In Every Generation, German Militarism has Overrun Other Peoples' Homes, Burning, Robbing and Killing!
We Must Protect Our Democracy, Our Homes and Our Children!
HELP FIGHT NAZISM!

At the time this postcard was published, America wanted no part of "Europe's war" but the card was thought-provoking and helped forge resentment toward Hitler, which was magnified two years later.

United States, published by New York International Workers Order Peace Committee, mailed August 1940.

The New York International Workers Order Peace Committee, in all certainty a Communist front organization, took a different tact than World Peace posters to keep America out of the war. While the former stressed the enormous cost of weapons, the latter featured photographic evidence of war's horrors. It's ironic that both the left wing Soviet partisans and the right wing fascist sympathizers wanted to see America stay out of the war in the beginning. These unlikely allies had formed a non-aggression pact in 1939 and divided Poland between them. Communist Russia and Nazi Germany were perpetrating most of the horrific aspects of the war the N.Y.I.W.O.P.C. claimed it wanted to prevent. Groups like this were very well organized.

This postcard was sent August 20, 1940, to New York Senator Robert F. Wagner with the following message: "Sir: Please be advised that peacetime military conscription is abhorrent to me as to millions of Americans regardless of whatever type of revision, concession or amendment (e.g. the Maloney amendment)." Naturally, the abhorrence people like this had to military conscription instantly evaporated when Germany attacked Russia. Then they couldn't wait for America to involve itself as Russia's ally.

The futuristic art of Gyula Zilzer, this example titled "Fascism Means War," was converted into postcards in four languages (English, German, French, and Spanish) and published by American Representative of Edition du Carrefour Paris located at 38 Union Square in New York City. Many left wing and Communist organizations in the Union Square area churned out anti-Nazi and anti-Fascist material prior to the war. Note the bloated capitalist providing sustenance through a feeding tube to the Nazi driving the mechanized vehicle that is destroying everything in its path. Zilzer's brilliant portrayal of Fascism-Nazism even includes bombers and hanged victims to capture many of the horrific ingredients of the war about to come. The plutocratic "Daddy Warbucks" has a long history in Marxist propaganda, and the new horrors of industrial warfare, here a mechanized "Grim Reaper," which parodies farm machinery, became standard anti-war imagery following the First World War.

United States, by Gyula Zilzer, published by American Representative of Edition du Carrefour Paris, Union Square, NY, value $25-$50.

"Dick" was taking a cruise on the Panama line to Haiti in September 1940 when he sketched this artistic commentary on the war. Hitler had said he'd be in London on August 15, so the Nazi warlord is pacing nervously with sweat coming from his brow. Already August 15 has been scratched out. So has September 1. A new date of October 1 is posted with the comment, "Oh! Der Tag!" (Oh! The day!). The day never came. Dick's foray into the world of cartoon art may have ended with this postcard or he may have made it a career. But like millions of others, he sent the war home on a postcard. In a popular enterprise (and the war effort became very popular), individuals need not wait for commercial or official propaganda. They create a genuine popular art form. Unfortunately, few good examples are extant and they are highly valued by collectors. A 1993-94 exhibit at the Imperial War Museum in London entitled "Forces Sweethearts: Wartime Romance from the First World War to the Gulf" featured a number of hand-drawn cards from a British soldier named Alf Simpson. Remarkably, some of these amateur efforts are much more clever than the postcards that seem to echo the same idea, (in the case of postcards, bodily functions) over and over again.

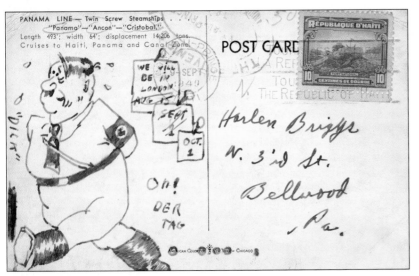

Original art, by "Dick," mailed from Port au Prince, Haiti, September 1940, value $25-$50.

A NATION UNITED IN DEFENSE CANNOT FAIL

"Nazi agents, propagandists, defeatists and dupes preach "peace—peace" in the same way the devil quotes scripture. But, actually they are serving the most brutal warmongers of all time."
Franklin D. Roosevelt,
Jackson Day Dinner, March, 1941

United States, published by Artvue Postcard Co., New York, 1941, value $50 and up.

These extremely rare and interesting cards published by the Artvue Postcard Co. of New York fall more into the political category than war propaganda. However, they are included because they set the tone for events to come. The first card, "A Nation United in Defense Cannot Fail," pictures 1940 presidential opponents Republican Wendell Willkie and President Franklin Roosevelt shaking hands. Wilkie is saying, "Our Country is in danger, No time for partizanship (sic)," while Roosevelt replies, "Very Well, Wendell Willkie." A map of the United States surrounding the two leaders is composed of applauding citizens. A quote from Roosevelt's Jackson Day dinner speech in March 1941 appears at the bottom: "Nazi Agents, propagandists, defeatists and dupes preach 'peace-peace' in the same way the devil quotes scripture. But, actually they are serving the most brutal warmongers of all time."

The second card depicts the great American hero Charles Lindbergh as a Nazi. It shows Hitler, Hess, Goebbels, and Goering proclaiming, "Our Future Gauleiter in America" while listening to a Lindbergh radio speech. Lindbergh did indeed visit Germany in 1936, coming away highly impressed by their military might and advocating that America not get involved in a future war with them. This opinion was shared by a majority of Americans. Lindbergh was a prominent member of the America First Committee, as were many patriotic Americans such as Senator Burton Wheeler of Montana and Col. Robert McCormick, publisher of the *Chicago Tribune*. Roosevelt hated Lindbergh and did everything possible to discredit him. Despite anti-Lindbergh postcards like this, obviously produced by Roosevelt supporters, the first man to fly across the Atlantic remains a great American hero and was a patriotic American his entire life.

United States, published by Artvue Postcard Co., New York, 1941.

United States, published by the Brussels Restaurant, New York.

"The Oldest Citizen of Brussels," a famous statue known as the Mannekin Pis located near the Brussels Market Place, shows total disdain for Hitler, who goose steps through the shower on this imaginative advertising postcard for the Brussels Restaurant, 26 East 63rd St., New York City. According to the back of the card, "The story of the legend is that at the beginning of the 17th century a little boy was lost. When his father finally found him he built a statue depicting the child in the exact pose in which he was discovered."

This card dates itself to the time before May 1940 when Belgium was overrun by the Nazis because on the back it says of the young boy, "He has all the uniforms of the Allied countries and he wears them on their national day. On the 4th of July he wears an American uniform and medals."

Comic postcards featuring the Mannekin Pis performing have been produced for years, and during World War II Hitler was a ripe candidate for spraying. Cherubim or innocent little boys making water are standard features of European fountains; in the United States, it is commonly spitting dolphins or fish. American postcard propaganda regularly employs a dog lifting his leg on Hitler or other objects of disrespect.

The bestial portrayal of the Axis leaders as dogs, monkeys, snakes, and other animals was used frequently by American artists to vilify the enemy. M. Rosenstein of Lancaster, Pennsylvania, produced this card casting Mussolini, Hirohito, and Hitler (left to right) as "Three Dirty Dogs" while evoking America's battle cry, "Remember Pearl Harbor." After Japan's attack on Pearl Harbor December 7, 1941, a reeling America, unprepared for war and with much of its fleet destroyed, was able to retaliate with little more than slogans for nearly a year until America's war production moved into high gear. More than any American World War II slogan, "Remember Pearl Harbor" rallied a nation to avenge the sneak attack and gain the ultimate victory.

United States, by M. Rosenstein, published by M. Rosenstein, 1941.

United States, by Seymour R. Goff, published by House of Seagram, NY, 1941, value $25-$50.

United States, by Seymour R. Goff, published by House of Seagram, NY, 1941, value $25-$50.

While it might be assumed that postcards and posters are first cousins and that the postcard is often nothing more than a mailable version of the former, this was not commonly the case during World War II. To be sure, there were notable exceptions; this group of images had wide distribution in both forms.

In many respects the House of Seagram was clairvoyant. They foresaw the United States involvement in World War II at least three months before Pearl Harbor was attacked by Japan. In September 1941 they began running magazine and newspaper ads imploring Americans to "Buy War Bonds and Stamps" before they bought luxuries such as Seagram's own alcoholic beverages. One famous Seagram ad was headlined "We Don't Want Bond Money." And they were fortunate enough to have Seymour R. Goff as their art director. Goff, a graduate of the Massachusetts School of Art in Boston, often signed his work Essargee after his initials S.R.G. He was a brilliant poster artist, comparable to any in the world. Before the war he had worked in sales promotion creating window displays for the Seagram brands. He originated and did the artwork for Seagram's wartime advertising campaign labeled "Hush-Hush," warning Americans about the danger of loose talk in wartime.

Less than two weeks after Pearl Harbor, the House of Seagram began shipping Goff's posters and postcards to thousands of taverns and package stores, as well as to military bases, clubs, hotels, and federal, state, and municipal offices throughout North America - more than 500,000 in all. Goff's images also appeared on special propaganda stamps affixed to the backs of letters and on cards folded into an inverted-V and placed on tabletops (these are known as table tents in the restaurant trade). The four Goff postcards distributed by Seagram's appear here (see page 20 also).

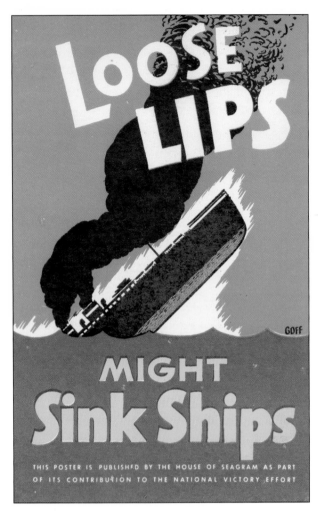

United States, by Seymour R. Goff, published by House of Seagram, NY, 1941, value $25-$50.

United States, by Seymour R. Goff, published by House of Seagram, NY, 1941, value $25-$50.

Carlton Waugh was a gifted editorial cartoonist for the *New York World and Tribune* in the 1920s before embarking on a career as a comic strip artist (*Dickie Dare,* which he took over from Milton Caniff of *Terry and the Pirates* fame and *Hank,* among others). He injected social consciousness into his art. The son of the famous seascape artist Frederick Waugh, Carlton Waugh gave up writing comic strips in 1945 to write his history of the art, *The Comics,* which was published in 1947.

This dramatic postcard titled "We Must Rescue Christmas Itself," produced for the Committee to Defend America in early December 1941, shows a mother holding her baby, another daughter holding a Christmas tree aloft, and the father hanging on desperately to a life raft as rescue ships speed toward them. The legend on the back of the card is as forthright as Waugh's art: "This year we cherish Christmas more than ever before. All that it means of good will among men, of striving toward peace, of untrammeled worship of God, of free enjoyment, of fear-free companionship with those we love, is dear to us now, when it is in peril. Let us take courage for the work and sacrifice necessary to rescue Christmas itself from the dark forces which would destroy it." The prayerful message was quite appropriate at the time. Beginning with the attack on Pearl Harbor, the Japanese "ran wild" in the Pacific, defeating their enemies with ease and brutality. It was a vast gamble, however, because as Admiral Yamamoto well knew when planning the opening strike, if the Americans didn't give up quickly, Japan would in the end be defeated. Until the battle of Midway, propaganda was the main American weapon of war.

WE MUST RESCUE CHRISTMAS ITSELF

United States, by Carlton Waugh, published by Committee to Defend America, mailed December 22, 1941, value $25-$50.

Albert Herman's direct and brutal postcard was produced shortly after Japan's attack on Pearl Harbor. The poetic caption, "Let's Bury the Hatchet in Hitler's Neck to Sink the Rising Sun," inverts Hollywood Indian-lingo for peacemaking, and the graphic shows a decapitated Hitler whose corpse has produced a river of blood, obliterating the Rising Sun of Japan's flag. The image captures Allied strategy: commit the bulk of American resources to the European war first because Germany, the stronger enemy, might never be beaten if she gained total control of the continent, and then finish off Japan. Popular hatred of Japan, exacerbated by the sneak attack and the revelation of the Pacific war's brutality, caused much sentiment for direct action and a quick march to Tokyo. This was encouraged by the Navy and by General MacArthur, neither expecting a large role in a European war, by what was perceived as Britain's primary interest in protecting her Empire and financial interests, and by the fact that Hitler's main opponent, the USSR, was not universally loved. Herman's postcard is, however, prophetic and the strategy was sound.

United States, by Albert Herman, 1941, value $25-$50.

Although the war was going badly for the United States in early 1942 when Paul Frederick Berdanier produced this artwork for United Features Syndicate, he correctly prophesied that American production would indeed turn the war in the Allies' favor. Borrowing from the Otto Harbach-Jerome Kern song "Smoke Gets In Your Eyes" from the 1933 Broadway show *Roberta*, Berdanier shows smoke belching from American factories, bringing tears to the eyes of the typical propaganda stereotyped weak-eyed, bucktoothed Japanese. Part of a highly desirable eight-card set by Colourpicture of Boston, the postcard below epitomizes the brilliance of Berdanier's work. Winner of numerous awards for his cartoon art, Berdanier remained active with United Features Syndicate until four years before his death in 1961 at the age of 83. Illustrated here are all eight cards in the set (pages 22 to 25).

United States, by Paul Frederick Berdanier, a Colourpicture Publication by Contemporary Cartoons, NY, 1942, value $50 and up.

United States, by Paul Frederick Berdanier, a Colourpicture Publication by Contemporary Cartoons, NY, 1942, value $50 and up.

*United States, by Paul Frederick Berdanier, a
Colourpicture Publication by Contemporary Cartoons,
NY, 1942, value $50 and up.*

*United States, by Paul Frederick Berdanier, a
Colourpicture Publication by Contemporary Cartoons,
NY, 1942, value $50 and up.*

*United States, by Paul Frederick Berdanier, a
Colourpicture Publication by Contemporary Cartoons,
NY, 1942, value $50 and up.*

*United States, by Paul Frederick Berdanier, a
Colourpicture Publication by Contemporary Cartoons,
NY, 1942, value $50 and up.*

United States, by Paul Frederick Berdanier, a Colourpicture Publication by Contemporary Cartoons, NY, 1942, value $50 and up.

United States, by Paul Frederick Berdanier, a Colourpicture Publication by Contemporary Cartoons, NY, 1942, value $50 and up.

If an artist can be called a genius, Arthur Szyk (pronounced Shick) was indeed such a man. His amazingly detailed caricatures created with numerous vibrant colors set him apart from all other artists of his day. Employing a miniaturist style of art that dates back to the 16th century, Szyk was at his best during World War II.

His anti-Axis art so infuriated Hitler, the German leader is said to have put a personal price on his head. President Roosevelt's wife Eleanor called him a "one-man army against Hitler." Using his pen as a sword, Szyk fought against all the tyrants of the world and never lost a battle. Many art scholars consider him the greatest 20th century illuminator.

Born in Lodz, Poland, in 1894, then part of Russia, he went to art school in Paris at the age of 15 but was drafted into the Russian army during World War I where he fought in the trenches. Moving back to Paris prior to World War II, he relocated in London in the late 1930s. Already gaining an international reputation, his illustration of the *Haggadah* was called by the *Times of London*, "worthy of being considered among the most beautiful books ever produced by the hand of man." In 1939 British authorities persuaded Szyk to relocate to the still neutral United States to sway American public opinion against the Nazis, and he was extremely successful in doing so. Landing a job as editorial cartoonist for the *New York Post*, his anti-Nazi cartoons frequently appeared on the front page. His finest anti-Axis work also graced the covers of such magazines as *Esquire, Time,* and *Colliers* and another newspaper, *The Chicago Sun.* A 1941 survey conducted by *Esquire* magazine claimed Szyk's political cartoons were even more popular with young American military trainees than photos of movie actresses or pinup girls. They must have believed their survey because *Esquire* published this six-card set (pages 26 to 28) featuring some of Szyk's most brilliant work. Becoming an American citizen in 1948, Arthur Szyk died in New Canaan, Connecticut, of a heart attack in 1951 at the age of 57.

"DECEMBER 7, 1941"

United States, by Arthur Szyk, published by Esquire, *1942, value $50 and up.*

THE NEW ORDERLIES

United States, by Arthur Szyk, published by Esquire, *1942, value $50 and up.*

United States, by Arthur Szyk, published by Esquire, *1942, value $50 and up.*

United States, by Arthur Szyk, published by Esquire, *1942, value $50 and up.*

THE MAP MAKER

United States, by Arthur Szyk, published by Esquire, *1942, value $50 and up.*

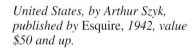

United States, by Arthur Szyk, published by Esquire, *1942, value $50 and up.*

"This damn winter is just another intrigue of Roosevelt and the international bankers"

DETOUR ON THE GLORY ROAD

The armed forces took advantage of the skills of their personnel by encouraging them to practice their art while serving their country. Bill Mauldin, Dave Breger, and George Baker are excellent examples, having created Willie and Joe, Private Breger, and the Sad Sack, respectively. Far less known is Private Dick Bothwell, who produced works like this postcard entitled "Special Delivery from the USA." Produced early in the war, it calls attention to Col. James H. Doolittle's raid on Tokyo and other sites on the Japanese mainland on April 18, 1942, staged a little over four months after Pearl Harbor. The Doolittle Raid, not made public in the United States until the second week in May, proved that Japan was vulnerable from the air.

United States, by Dick Bothwell, published by Observer Printing House, Charlotte, NC, 1942.

United States, by A.J. Metcalfe, published by Metcalfe, 1942, mailed October 1943.

Numerous World War II propaganda postcards tied buying war bonds with the ultimate defeat of the Axis powers. A.J. Metcalfe's postcard depicts a triple-headed sea serpent bearing the likenesses of Hitler, Tojo, and Mussolini hunted down by a Coast Guard cutter and a Navy destroyer with the message, "You Buy the Bonds, We'll Clear the Ponds." The commander of the Coast Guard cutter is flipping a coin and hollering, "I'll match you for it Admiral." Though coastal blackouts were more effective against U-boats than was the Coast Guard, the Battle of the North Atlantic was vital to the Allies and was popular in the war effort.

29

United States, by Walter Wellman, A Colourpicture Publication, Cambridge, MA, Morale Builders Series A.

Walter Wellman's first foray into political cartooning occurred prior to World War I when he did a series of postcards on women's suffrage, so he was in the twilight of his career when he did the anti-Hitler postcard above for Colourpicture Productions of Cambridge, Massachusetts. His scrawled signature trademark in the lower right-hand corner identifies another Walter Wellman gem. A moon-faced soldier in World War I doughboy garb gives Hitler a nose thumb salute guaranteed to boost morale and bring a smile to the troops in training far from their loved ones back home. Also shown here are the other three cards in the "Morale Builder Series."

United States, by Walter Wellman, A Colourpicture Publication, Cambridge, MA, Morale Builders Series A.

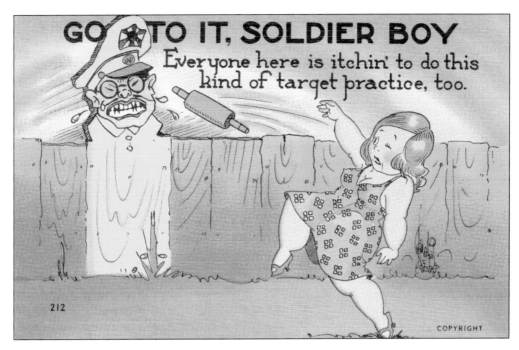

United States, by Walter Wellman, A Colourpicture Publication, Cambridge, MA, Morale Builders Series A.

United States, by Walter Wellman, A Colourpicture Publication, Cambridge, MA, Morale Builders Series A.

United States, by Walter Munson, published by Tichnor Brothers, Boston, MA, 1942.

Although Adolph Hitler was singled out more than any other Axis leader to bear the brunt of American propaganda, there was considerably more animosity directed at the Japanese people than at the German people. This was due mainly to the fact that it was the Japanese who struck the first blow against the United States by bombing Pearl Harbor. It was invariably termed a "sneak attack." Racial prejudice toward the Japanese - including the 125,000 of Japanese birth or descent on American soil - intensified into rage after Pearl Harbor and quickly eclipsed any such general feelings towards the Germans, except for Der Fuehrer himself. It was almost as if the United States had two enemies: Hitler and the Japanese.

Two sets of postcards published by Tichnor Brothers of Boston bear this out (pages 32 to 38). The "Hitler Comics" had five designs while the "Jap Comics" had ten. On the card above, Walt Munson, famous for the cherub-like features of his characters, shows a soldier pulling up his pants after defecating in a chamber pot bearing Hitler's likeness. Card #1 in the "Jap Comics" series (page 36) shows the long arm of Uncle Sam administering a crushing blow on the stereotype Japanese while Tokyo is being bombed in the background. Both sets were published early in the war in 1942.

United States, by Walter Munson, published by Tichnor Brothers, Boston, MA, 1942.

United States, by Walter Munson, published by Tichnor Brothers, Boston, MA, 1942.

United States, by Walter Munson, published by Tichnor Brothers, Boston, MA, 1942.

United States, by Walter Munson, published by Tichnor Brothers, Boston, MA, 1942.

United States, by Walter Munson, published by Tichnor Brothers, Boston, MA, 1942.

United States, by Walter Munson, published by Tichnor Brothers, Boston, MA, 1942.

United States, by Walter Munson, published by Tichnor Brothers, Boston, MA, 1942.

United States, by Walter Munson, published by Tichnor Brothers, Boston, MA, 1942.

United States, by Walter Munson, published by Tichnor Brothers, Boston, MA, 1942.

United States, by Walter Munson, published by Tichnor Brothers, Boston, MA, 1942.

United States, by Walter Munson, published by Tichnor Brothers, Boston, MA, 1942.

United States, by Walter Munson, published by Tichnor Brothers, Boston, MA, 1942.

United States, by Walter Munson, published by Tichnor Brothers, Boston, MA, 1942.

United States, by Walter Munson, published by Tichnor Brothers, Boston, MA, 1942.

United States, by Reg Manning, published by Curteich,
Chicago, distributed by Lollesgard Speciality Co., Tucson.

The famous Arizona cartoonist Reg Manning contributed to America's propaganda war effort with some of the most imaginative postcards issued during World War II. For the United States, the first major piece of good news in the Pacific war took place on April 10, 1942, when 16 B-25 medium bombers commanded by Col. Jimmy Doolittle took off from the deck of the aircraft carrier *Hornet* and bombed Tokyo, some 670 miles away. Although the bomb damage was minimal, it had a tremendous psychological effect on the Japanese, who until then felt they were impervious to attack from America. American satisfaction with the success was vastly out of proportion to its military value. Shortly after the attack, Manning seized on the news of the Doolittle Raid and came up with this brilliant depiction of the fictional Admiral Motomissin (as in "Motor Missing") deploring, "Oh Son of Heaven! Snap the sacred Kimono! American Planes Coming! Run for the Shelter!" Admiral Motomissin is followed closely by little Itchy Itchy carrying the Hara-Kiri (suicide) sword. As always in propaganda postcards, the Japanese are depicted as heavily bespectacled, diminutive, and bucktoothed, though the admiral depicted here is uncharacteristically built like the caricature Goering, who was in reality between beefy and obese. The postcard title, "The Yanks Are Coming!" is that of the most popular American World War I song. As an artist, Manning was in the same class as fellow editorial cartoonists Arthur Szyk and Paul Frederick Berdanier. His other anti-Axis cards shown on page 40 show how skilled he truly was.

United States, by Reg Manning, published by Curteich, Chicago, distributed by Lollesgard Speciality Co., Tucson.

United States, by Reg Manning, published by Curteich, Chicago, distributed by Lollesgard Speciality Co., Tucson.

United States, by Reg Manning, published by Curteich, Chicago, distributed by Lollesgard Speciality Co., Tucson.

Fertile imaginations were not lacking in World War II postcard art. This postcard, produced by Babcock & Borough of Albuquerque, New Mexico, shows the hide of a Japanese soldier branded with the message, "Made in Japan, Caught in the Pacific, Tanned in the U.S.A., So Solly." The legend on the back features the following poem: "Here Hangs the Pelt of a Jap, Who Mistook a Yank for a Sap, He never deserved to be preserved, So we just kept his hide and his cap."

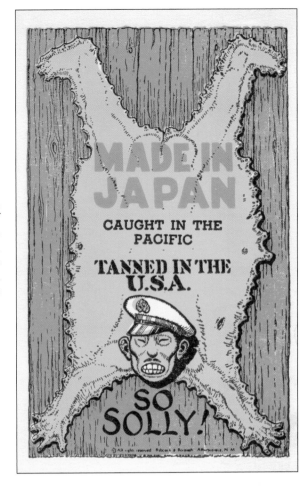

United States, published by Babcock & Borough, postmarked September 7, 1942.

Hitler bit off more than he could chew when he invaded Russia on June 22, 1941. Although German forces advanced quickly during the early stages of the campaign, they bogged down completely when ferocious and gallant defenses around Moscow, Stalingrad, and Leningrad, aided by an extremely severe Russian winter, halted the advance. This imaginative postcard published by Metropolitan Post Card Co. of Everett, Massachusetts, shows Hitler scrambling back to Germany pursued by the Russian bear who has taken a bite out of his pants, exposing his bare behind. It's an excellent play on words by the unknown artist as he titles the card "Dere Goebels (both words misspelled) Der Huntin' here is Terrible. Here iss (sic) me Mitt a Bare Behind." Even funnier, the artist pretends that Hitler has gone to Russia on a hunting trip and is sending this image as a vacation postcard to his propaganda minister, Joseph Goebbels, back in Germany.

United States, artist unknown, published by Metropolitan Post Card Co., Everett, MA.

United States, value $25-$50.

This four-card series remains a complete mystery, although it is one of the truly outstanding propaganda postcard sets of World War II. Not only is the brilliant artist not identified, but also no publisher is listed. It's obvious the unknown artist had a comic strip background and he had an excellent grasp of the events that were taking place, as well as a terrific imagination. The cards are extremely difficult to find, with "Dangerous Sailing" the least likely to turn up. Most often they are found unused, but I have seen one card with a Ft. Meade, Maryland, postmark from 1942, which may mean it was sold in the Post Exchange there. It's fruitless to speculate because there are no definitive clues to go on. There is one certainty - these are among the best propaganda postcards produced during the war. Perhaps a reader will be able to solve the mystery. If you have any information, please contact Ron Menchine, PO Box 1, Long Green, MD 21092. The four cards are: "Allies to the Rescue," "Dangerous Sailing," "Slap the Jap Off the Map," and "The Last Roundup."

United States, value $25-$50.

United States, value $25-$50.

United States, value $25-$50.

United States, by Max Halverson, published by Beals, Des Moines, IA.

Without question the most prolific postcard publisher churning out propaganda color postcards was Beals of Des Moines, Iowa. Founded by Guy C. Beals in the mid-1920s as a small printing firm, by 1941 Beals was Iowa's largest lithographer and a national publisher of quality postcards. Their Art Tone "Glo Var" finished cards, an exclusive Beals process, used the talented artist Max Halverson to do all their anti-Axis cards. Halverson did a total of 16 different images demeaning the various Axis leaders, Hitler, Mussolini, and Hirohito (pages 44 to 50). While most concentrated on Hitler, there were seven that lambasted all three. Halverson's art featured extremely colorful images such as multi-colored uniforms on the terrible trio and exaggerated rosy cheeks on the United States soldiers and WACs who were humiliating Hitler and his cohorts. The WAC series was also distributed by the Asheville Postcard Co. in North Carolina but manufactured by Beals. One of the features of this book is to identify all known anti-Axis cards produced by the major publishers.

United States, by Max Halverson, published by Beals, Des Moines, IA.

United States, by Max Halverson, published by Beals, Des Moines, IA.

United States, by Max Halverson, published by Beals, Des Moines, IA.

United States, by Max Halverson, published by Beals, Des Moines, IA.

United States, by Max Halverson, published by Beals, Des Moines, IA.

United States, by Max Halverson, published by Beals, Des Moines, IA.

United States, by Max Halverson, published by Beals, Des Moines, IA.

United States, by Max Halverson, published by Beals, Des Moines, IA.

United States, by Max Halverson,
published by Beals, Des Moines, IA.

United States, by Max Halverson, published by Beals, Des Moines, IA.

United States, by Max Halverson,
published by Beals, Des Moines, IA.

United States, by Max Halverson, published by Beals, Des Moines, IA.

United States, by Max Halverson, published by Beals, Des Moines, IA.

United States, by Max Halverson, published by Beals, Des Moines, IA, distributed by Asheville Postcard Co., NC.

United States, by Max Halverson, published by Beals, Des Moines, IA, distributed by Asheville Postcard Co., NC.

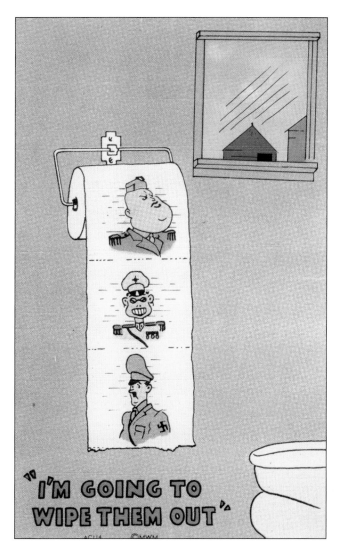

United States, published by Midwest Map Co., Aurora, MO.

Midwest Map Co. of Aurora, Missouri, produced one of the few color scatological cards showing images of Mussolini, Tojo, and Hitler on toilet paper with the title "I'm Going to Wipe Them Out." Most of the scatological humor was confined to black and white cards often sent inside envelopes, so this was considered somewhat adventuresome on Midwest Map's part in the 1940s. The other cards produced by MWM were considerably milder (pages 52 to 53). One shows a dreaming GI kicking Hitler in the rear end with the caption "He Has A Kick Coming - I'm Going To See He Gets It." Number AV 210 shows a United States plane downing two Japanese Zeros with the clever title "Blackout of the Rising Sun," referring to Japan being the "land of the rising sun." Fertile imaginations were certainly not lacking during World War II.

There's nothing very subtle about the card entitled "Bundles for Hirohito," as a GI carries a huge bomb destined for Japan. The fifth, "Wanted, Big Reward Offered, I'm Coming Home Rich," shows a soldier with a bayonet and pictures of the three Axis leaders. The final two are "Boy! We Get More Darn Subs This Way" and "This Production Line's Gettin' Too Fast For Me!"

United States, published by Midwest Map Co., Aurora, MO.

United States, published by Midwest Map Co., Aurora, MO.

United States, published by Midwest Map Co., Aurora, MO.

United States, published by Midwest Map Co., Aurora, MO.

United States, published by Midwest Map Co., Aurora, MO.

United States, published by Midwest Map Co., Aurora, MO.

United States, published by Mid States Press, Chicago, 1942.

Mid States Press, located in Chicago, decided to pay homage to all branches of the United States armed forces: Army, Navy, Air Force, and Marines. It's the only set that devotes one card to each branch of the service. Another unique feature of the series has the art taking up half the stamp side of the card, leaving the other side to send a more detailed message. Whereas the various governments produced many propaganda postcards during World War II, all United States cards were privately produced. As a result, there is more variety among United States cards. In this series, the Army card shows a soldier chasing Hitler with a bayonet. The Navy card has a sailor banging Hitler's and Mussolini's heads together. The Air Force pilot is dropping Tojo, Mussolini, and Hitler as human bombs on Axis territory, and the Marine is putting the Japanese soldier through a clothes wringer. Before the advent of the dryer, the clothes wringer was an integral part of every American household, although virtually non-existent today.

United States, published by Mid States Press, Chicago, 1942.

United States, published by Mid States Press, Chicago, 1942.

United States, published by Mid States Press, Chicago, 1942.

United States, by Paris, published by E.C. Kropp, Milwaukee, WI, mailed December 1942.

"Keep 'Em Flying!" was a popular expression: keep Allied planes in the air for use against the Axis. Using it as a double entendre, the artist who signs his name Paris shows Uncle Sam booting three Japanese soldiers in the rear, sending them flying head over heels. Although Hitler was the individual focal point of most World War II propaganda, Japan and its people were favored by postcard artists in the United States. This is probably due to two main factors. There were many more Americans of German descent in the United States than Japanese-Americans, and it was the Japanese who struck the first blow against the United States in World War II when they attacked Pearl Harbor. Put another way, America has a sturdy tradition of racism which found a universally approved outlet in Japan, while American forces were steadily (and not always successfully) engaged in difficult, brutal, and often loathsome combat with the Japanese, beginning on December 8, 1941. Both are apparent in postcard iconography.

The Japanese depicted in this postcard are particularly small and rodent-like, balling up when kicked. What is fascinating is to compare the Japanese characterized by American cartoonists during the war and those who were drawn after the war, during the Occupation and during the early 1950s when Japan was the main venue for GIs taking R&R (Rest and Relaxation). One American cartoonist, Bill Hume, produced a series of cartoon books for American servicemen, *Babysan: A Private Look at the Japanese Occupation*, and *The Hume'n Slant on Japan*, in which all of the women are Japanese and they are uniformly buxom, sexy, and wearing Western hairstyles. Few are short, none wear glasses or sport buckteeth and all look remarkably like Japanese-American bobby-soxers. During the Korean War, Hume's renderings of idealized Japanese women are used as pinups by GIs in the Far East just like the *Esquire* pinups by Vargas and Petty had been used during the war. Paris, who was E.C. Kropp's most prolific anti-Axis artist, also did these cards for the publisher.

United States, by Paris, published by E.C. Kropp, Milwaukee, WI, mailed December 1942.

United States, by Paris, published by E.C. Kropp, Milwaukee, WI, mailed December 1942.

United States, by Paris, published by E.C. Kropp, Milwaukee, WI, mailed December 1942.

United States, by Paris, published by E.C. Kropp, Milwaukee, WI, mailed December 1942.

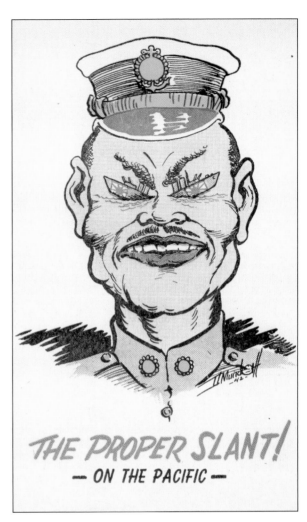

United States, by D. Mundorf, published by Kahuna Komics, Honolulu, 1942, value $25-$50.

United States, probably by D. Mundorf, published by Kahuna Komics, Honolulu, 1942, value $25-$50.

Hawaiian cartoonist D. Mundorf plays with an old slur in his work "The Proper Slant!" by showing a Japanese naval officer with "slant eyes" represented by sinking Japanese ships. United States submarines were known as the "Silent Service" and they sank more Japanese ships than all other sea and air units combined. In 1943, shortly after this postcard was issued, the Silent Service sank 22 enemy warships and 296 merchant vessels, literally strangling Japan's Pacific lifeline. Without being able to supply shipments of food and materials to their far-flung outposts, the Japanese were unable to retain territory won early in the war.

The imaginative card at left, also published by Kahuna Komics and titled "A Royal Flush for Hirohito," shows Uncle Sam flushing the Japanese fleet down the toilet. Though not signed, the image is probably another Mundorf gem.

United States, by Charles Heath, 1942, not postally used.

A good camera, a few feet of space, a well trained dog, and some American imagination were all that was required to churn out effective anti-Axis propaganda postcards. Los Angeles photographer Charles Heath and entrepreneur H. Wachtman, plus a spotted dog with a harness combined to produce numerous amusing scatological photographic postcards. The thoughtfully discriminating dog was the focal point, and lifted his leg at such headlines as "What the U.S.A. Thinks of the Dirty Japs" and "This Is What We Think of the Hitler Gang" that appeared in the bogus newspaper, *Hollywood Press*. The dog was also photographed seated on a chamber pot labeled variously "Collection for Hitler," "Help Hitler War Fund," and "Donations for Japs," among others. The same cards on printed rather than photographic stock appeared with a 1942 copyright for the Zipper Novelty & Joke Shop of Los Angeles printed in the bottom white border. Thus even man's best friend aided the war effort.

United States, by Charles Heath, 1942, not postally used.

United States, by Charles Heath, 1942, not postally used.

United States, by Charles Heath, 1942, not postally used.

United States, by Charles Heath, 1942, not postally used.

United States, by Charles Heath, 1942, not postally used.

There were many postcards of the era that employed dogs urinating or defecating as part of the war effort. One common theme is a dog doing his business in a helmet or pot marked "Hitler War Fund," or "Donations for Japs," and the like as illustrated on page 61. A more literary version has a dog peeing on *Mein Kampf* and another using Hitler's beer glass. The most graphic of all of these is captioned "The Birth of the Swastika" and shows an exhausted pooch lying next to a Nazi symbol fashioned from steaming dog stools.

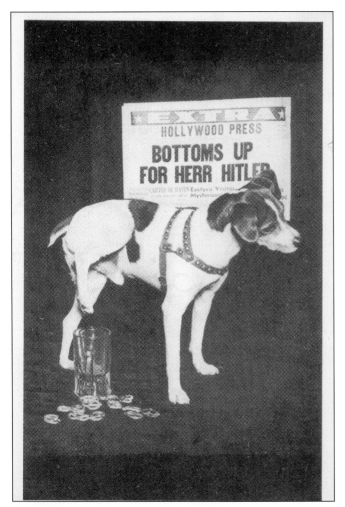

Publisher and artist unlisted.

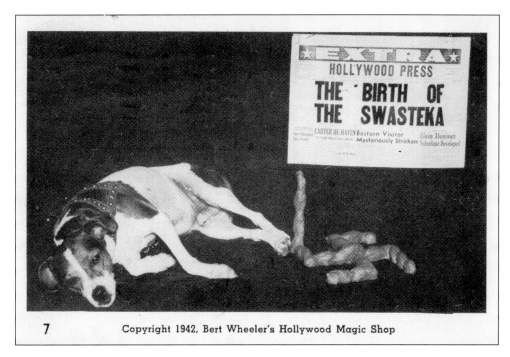

United States, published by Bert Wheeler's Hollywood Magic Shop, 1942.

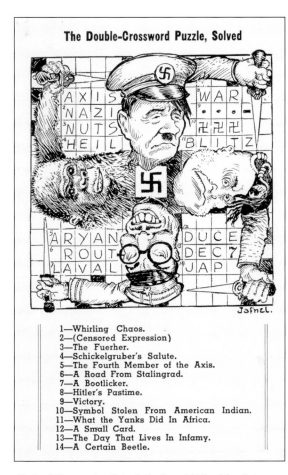

United States, by S.A. Jafnel, published by S.A. Jafnel.

Solving crossword puzzles has provided joy and amusement to millions over the years, and artist S.A. Jafnel cleverly solves his anti-Axis "Double Crossword Puzzle" featuring dagger-wielding Hitler, Mussolini, Tojo, and their natural ally, a gorilla (monster). Predictably, some of the definitions are genuinely witty; none show the slightest respect for the Axis. Another Jafnel postcard signed Jaf and titled "A Pain in the Axis" shows a caricature of Hitler guarding his rear and the poem, "I'm a wacky little Nazi, I soon may get the sack, I fear a second front the most when coming in the back." The second front for the Allies began November 7, 1942, with the invasion of North Africa.

The clues and answers in the solved crossword puzzle are: **Axis** Whirling Chaos; **Nazi** Censored Expression; **Nuts** The Fuehrer; **Heil** Schickelgruber's Salute; **Aryan** The Fourth Member of the Axis (just below the gorilla); **Route** A Road from Stalingrad; **Laval** (Vichy French Prime Minister) A Bootlicker; **War** Hitler's Pastime; **Victory; Swastika** Symbol Stolen from American Indian; **Blitz** What the Yanks Did in Africa; **Duce** (Mussolini) A Small Card; **Dec. 7** A Day That Will Live In Infamy; **Jap** A Certain Beetle.

Men Unashamed to Pray

We too must be unashamed
to pray — especially now.

This powerful postcard entitled "Men Unashamed to Pray" and mailed May 20, 1943, from Elmira, New York, carries the following printed message on the back: "Meeting of the SWAMS (Sweethearts, Wives and Mothers) at Trinity Parish House Wednesday, May 26 at 3 p.m. If you are a sweetheart, wife or mother of any of the 173 from Trinity in service, this means you. We need to make plans for the future. H. E. Hubbard."

All combatant nations enlisted God on their side. Even in Russia, where thousands of churches were closed under the fervently atheistic Stalin regime, the Soviet dictator had them reopened during World War II because he realized many citizens had a deep-rooted religious fervor that could not be obliterated, but might be drawn on in the desperate struggle. And although Hitler sent clerics to his notorious camps, he encouraged worship among his citizens. Japanese soldiers and subjects who would rather commit suicide than surrender considered their emperor divine. SWAMS waiting at home needed all the spiritual guidance and fellowship they could get to deal with the anxiety of loved ones sent far away, some never to return. This poignant graphic showing front line troops on their knees praying reminds those at home "We, too, must be unashamed to pray, especially now." These clean-cut, heroic, and dignified poses of fighting men, as depicted for home consumption, contrast strikingly with the Willie and Joe drawn by Bill Mauldin for the troops themselves.

United States, published by Trinity Parish House, Elmira, NY, mailed March 1943.

Wartime guests in The 23 Room, the cocktail lounge at the Hotel George Washington in New York City, could not only enjoy their favorite beverage, but have a good time solving the puzzle of putting two of the Axis leaders behind bars. Mussolini and Hitler appear on one side of the sheet and Tojo appears on the other with appropriate instructions to "Lock 'Em Up!" To add to the fun, the solution came with the following disclaimer: "To foil foreign agents, fifth columnists and spies, we printed the solution 'left-handed.' You can read it readily by holding it in front of a mirror." Incidentally, during the war years, "Rooms with tub, bath or shower" cost $2.50 and up. And this puzzle would be mailed courtesy of the Hotel George Washington. All you had to do was address it.

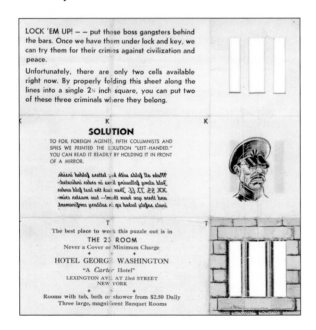

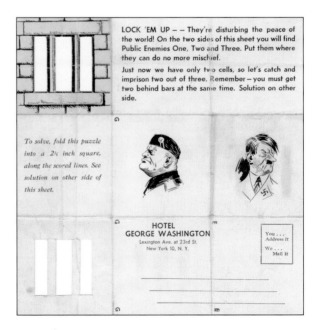

United States, published and distributed by George Washington Hotel, New York City.

United States, by Frederick Eichelbaum, Kansas City, MO, 1942, value $25-$50.

United States, by Henry Major, published by Bassons Dummy Products, 1943.

Frederick Eichelbaum, of Kansas City, Missouri, treated his friends to an unusual anti-Axis New Year's card in 1943. A caricature of Eichelbaum is kicking Tojo, Mussolini, and Hitler through a billboard for *Women's Wear Daily* with the message "Hey You! Here's Wishing You a New Year with a Happy Kick and a Helluva Kick for Schickelgruber and his Gas House Gang from Frederick Eichelbaum." In all probability Eichelbaum worked in the women's clothing field and used his clever card to show his patriotism as well as remind customers he was in business to serve them. During World War II, the United States was probably less divided than at any time in its history, with the entire nation working together to defeat the Axis powers. If they couldn't contribute on the battlefields, people felt they could at least show their support on the home front. Besides, postcards are both fun and inexpensive. If aiding the war effort helps your business, so much the better.

Artist Henry Major did a series of six cards called "Hex the Axis" for Bassons Dummy Products. Here we see Tojo, Mussolini, and Hitler singing "Where Do We Go From Here Boys, Where Do We Go From Here?" The answer lies below, as a smiling devil awaits their arrival in hell with a raised pitchfork (trident). Although many cards prophesied by verse that the Axis leaders would wind up in hell, this is the only known caricature of Satan, complete with horns beckoning "The Unholy Three" to their eternal home.

United States, published by D. Robbins & Co., New York City, 1943.

Although most of the World War II propaganda postcards produced in the United States were individual items, some were packaged as sets. This series entitled "Slam the Axis" (1943) was published by D. Robbins & Co., New York City. Each of the six cards (pages 66 to 68) features the message "For Victory, Buy United States War Bonds and Stamps." The card above, captioned "Fortune Teller: I See a Bad Finish for Your Rats," shows swami Uncle Sam gazing into a crystal ball which displays the message "Axis Defeat." Tojo, Hitler, and Mussolini are depicted as rats looking on with worried expressions. Their worries were justified as all three were dead by the end of 1945. Though the European dictators are clearly stupid, the Japanese warlord is typically a monster. The other five cards in the series are also pictured.

United States, published by D. Robbins & Co., New York City, 1943.

United States, published by D. Robbins & Co., New York City, 1943.

United States, published by D. Robbins & Co., New York City, 1943.

67

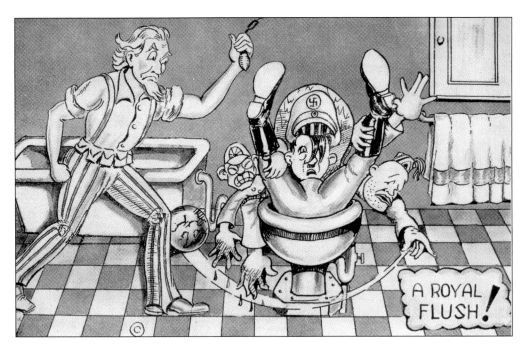

United States, published by D. Robbins & Co., New York City, 1943.

United States, published by D. Robbins & Co., New York City, 1943.

This elaborately designed card, which is part of the Axis Series produced by the Graphic Postcard Co. of New York, imitates a hunting license. Showing a snake whose head is a devilish Japanese caricature, the "Hunting License" reads, "Open Season on (sic) For Jap-Snakes. Will be recognized by that hissing s-s-s noise that sounds like 'So Sorry Please.' Warning - Do not turn your back as this animal is noted for Back Stabbing! Signed - Viper Exterminating Society." The "back stabbing" refers to the sneak attack on Pearl Harbor, December 7, 1941. Many American anti-Japanese propaganda postcards directly or indirectly referred to the Pearl Harbor attack, which instantly became a rallying cry throughout the United States for revenge against the Japanese. Eight of their scowling heads and a dozen rifles decorate the border filigree work.

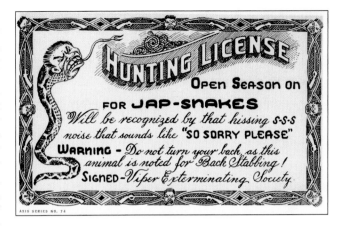

United States, published by Graphic Postcard Co., New York, Axis Series #74.

This photo montage of Hitler behind bars in prison garb is wittily cynical. The caption, "Quick! Get Cohen My Lawyer," shows Hitler, whose hatred of and unspeakable acts against Jews was unprecedented, demanding the best in legal assistance when he has been caught. Produced by the Hilborn Novelty Co. of New York City, the card is signed J.H., probably Mr. Hilborn himself. Jewish humor is frequently self-deprecating and this card is a classic example of how, by sometimes maintaining a bizarre sense of humor, Jewish culture has been able to survive despite horrendous atrocities perpetrated over centuries.

United States, by J.H., published by Hilborn Novelty Co., New York.

Borrowing the line "The Yanks are Coming" from George M. Cohan's famous World War I anthem "Over There," artist B.F. Long cleverly uses it as a theme for his postcard of Uncle Sam, the avuncular dentist inflicting serious but salutary pain on the Axis powers. During the early stages of America's entry into the war, it was "like pulling teeth" for the United States to gain a victory over the Japanese. It wasn't until June 3-6, 1942, during the Battle of Midway, considered by many to be the turning point in the Pacific war, that Uncle Sam defeated the Japanese for the first time. The turning point for Hitler came not at the hands of Uncle Sam, but of "Uncle Joe." During the winter of 1942-43 an army of over half a million Axis troops took at least 60% casualties in the Battle of Stalingrad.

United States, by B.F. Long, published by Graphic Postcard Co., New York.

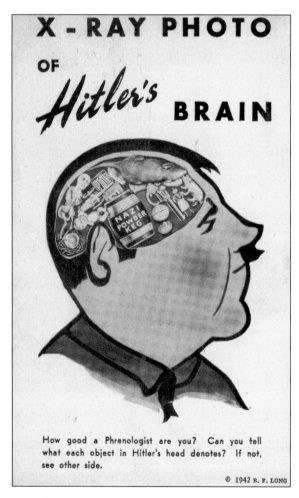

United States, by B.F. Long, published by Graphic Postcard Co., New York, 1942.

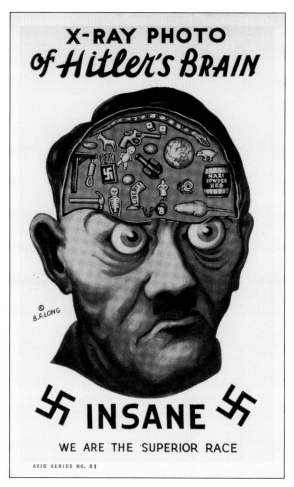

United States, by B.F. Long, published by Graphic Postcard Co., New York, 1942.

B.F. Long, one of World War II's most prolific propaganda postcard artists, possessed many attributes that made him successful: a vivid imagination, excellent drawing skills, and a marvelous sense of humor. Take "X-Ray Photo of Hitler's Brain" for example. Below the caricature of Hitler, Long asks, "How good a phrenologist are you? Can you tell what each object in Hitler's head denotes? If not, see other side." Long then identifies the various objects: "Rat: Has invaded and betrayed every country with which he had a peace pact. Matches: Has burned art and literature. Powder Keg: Has tried to blow civilization to pieces. Baby: Wants more babies for cannon fodder. Gun: Has a gun at the head of everyone in Europe. Pig: Wants to hog the world. Butcher: Wants to carve to pieces everyone who will not yield to him. Skeleton: Brings death and destruction. Cannon: Has slain innocent women and children. "'Haywire and Crack Pot' Nut: Fit subject for the 'bug house.'"

Considering Long produced this postcard in 1942 before many of the Nazi atrocities were widely known, it is indeed a classic in World War II propaganda and, sadly, most prophetic. It also, however, replays many of the standard propaganda accusations developed at length from the beginning of World War I.

Long also produced equally clever head graphics of Hirohito and Mussolini. Long's work was so well received by the people at the Graphic Postcard Co. in New York, they hired him to do many of their Axis Series postcards. They had him do a slightly different version of this card, which led off the Axis Series as card #51.

Much of the anti-Japanese propaganda art was directed against General Tojo rather than Emperor Hirohito. B.F. Long's "X-ray photo" of Hirohito's brain is one of the exceptions and shows no mercy, treating the Emperor with the same disdain usually reserved for Hitler and Mussolini. Among the discernible objects are a snake, skunk, beetle, sword, time bomb, revolver, handcuffs, monkey wrench, and skeleton. After the war, for the most part, Hirohito was held blameless for Japan's activities during the conflict and powerless to stop the militarists headed by Premier Tojo. However, some believe he could and should have exerted more influence and held the warlords in check. The delight of this anatomical psychoanalysis is not just in making the Divine Emperor into a thug, but in suggesting visually that he has ingested an entire novelty store that has gone to his head. While his brain contains all the delights a nine-year old boy could hope for, the look on his face is the usual sinister, inscrutable, and evil image that propaganda postcards give to the Japanese.

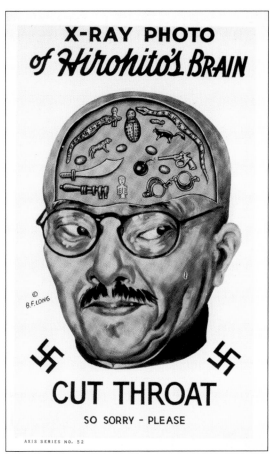

United States, by B.F. Long, published by Graphic Postcard Co., New York, card #52.

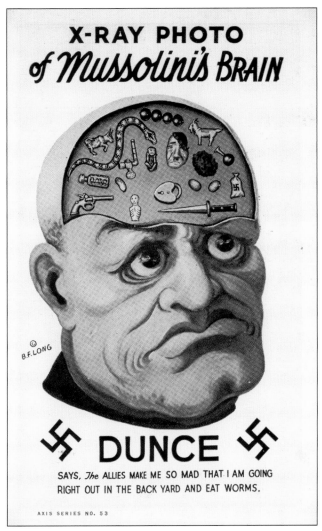

United States, by B.F. Long (Axis Series by B.F. Long, also by Joekerr), published by Graphic Postcard Co., New York.

Physiognomy can often play a pivotal role in how a person is perceived. Because of his large jutting jaw, Italy's El Duce, Benito Mussolini, was frequently depicted as a dunce and this is exactly how he is portrayed by Axis Series cartoonist B.F. Long in card #53 on page 71. Long previously lambasted Hitler and Hirohito, so the third member of the Axis leaders was fair game. Mussolini came to power in 1922 and many of his Fascist ideas were adopted by Hitler. Like Hitler, Mussolini was a spellbinding orator who drew hundreds of thousands during his outdoor speeches in Rome. The Italian leader relied on pageantry and spectacle to sway the masses just as Hitler did a few years later. Long dissected Mussolini's brain as containing such items as a snake, dagger, pistol, jackass, skeleton, and Hitler. The caption says, "The Allies make me so mad that I am going right out in the back yard and eat worms." Mussolini's end was a gruesome one, as he and Clara Petacci, his mistress, were caught by Italian partisans on April 28, 1945, while trying to escape to Switzerland. They were shot, their bodies mutilated and hung by the heels in Milan's main square.

The Graphic Postcard Co. of New York, who produced the Axis Series, was an extension of the Hilborn Novelty Co. that operated from the same address. In fact, several of the earlier Hilborn cards became part of the Axis Series. Thanks to Gilbert L. Pittman of Wichita, Kansas, and Roberta L. Greiner of Lady Lake, Florida, pages 73 to 82 show all the known cards in the Axis Series. You will note that several different images have the same number, probably because the series was updated. The numbers without a name may not have been issued or simply not seen or documented by any propaganda collectors.

51. X-Ray Photo Hitler's Brain
52. X-Ray Photo Hirohito's Brain
53. X-Ray Photo Mussolini's Brain
54. Mos-Cow
55. Two-Faced Pig
56. You Dirty Pig
57. We Are Going to Bury Hitler Face Down
58. Ready for the Dumps
58. The Yanks Are Coming
59. Hanging the Hangman
59. On Their Way to the Bug House (same as #77)
60. The Yanks Are Coming
60. Ready for the Dumps
61. No Pork Until These Pigs Are Killed
62. The Pot Brigade
63. Duck! Here Come the Allies
64.
65.
66.
67.
68.
69.
70. Heil Hitler
71. Ach du Lieber, Stop Pushin!
72. Celebration Day
73. A Bear Behind and a Terrible Future
74. Hunting License for Jap-Snakes
75. It Won't Be Long Now
76. I Feel Lousy with These Pests!
77. On Their Way to the Bug House (same as #59)
78. Mein Kampf - The End of This Story
79. Closing the Book
Different number series
A10. They Can't Strike Him Out!

United States, by B.F. Long (Axis Series by B.F. Long, also by Joekerr), published by Graphic Postcard Co., New York.

United States, by B.F. Long (Axis Series by B.F. Long), published by Graphic Postcard Co., New York.

United States, by B.F. Long (Axis Series by B.F. Long), published by Graphic Postcard Co., New York.

United States, by B.F. Long (Axis Series by B.F. Long), published by Graphic Postcard Co., New York.

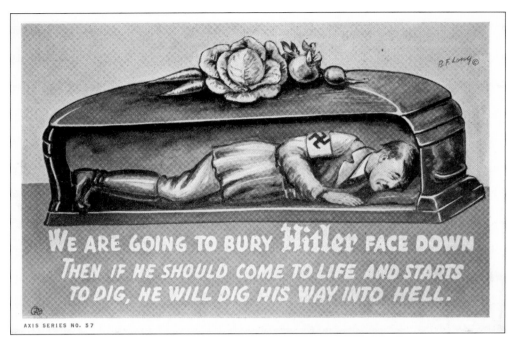

United States, by B.F. Long (Axis Series by B.F. Long), published by Graphic Postcard Co., New York.

United States, by B.F. Long (Axis Series by B.F. Long, also by Joekerr), published by Graphic Postcard Co., New York.

United States, by B.F. Long (Axis Series by B.F. Long, also by Joekerr), published by Graphic Postcard Co., New York.

United States, by B.F. Long (Axis Series by B.F. Long, also by Joekerr), published by Graphic Postcard Co., New York.

United States, by B.F. Long (Axis Series by B.F. Long, also by Joekerr), published by Graphic Postcard Co., New York.

United States, by B.F. Long (Axis Series by B.F. Long, also by Joekerr), published by Graphic Postcard Co., New York.

United States, by B.F. Long (Axis Series by B.F. Long, also by Joekerr), published by Graphic Postcard Co., New York.

United States, by B.F. Long (Axis Series by B.F. Long, also by Joekerr), published by Graphic Postcard Co., New York.

United States, by B.F. Long (Axis Series by B.F. Long, also by Joekerr), published by Graphic Postcard Co., New York.

United States, by B.F. Long (Axis Series by B.F. Long, also by Joekerr), published by Graphic Postcard Co., New York.

United States, by B.F. Long (Axis Series by B.F. Long, also by Joekerr), published by Graphic Postcard Co., New York.

United States, by B.F. Long (Axis Series by B.F. Long, also by Joekerr), published by Graphic Postcard Co., New York.

United States, by B.F. Long (Axis Series by B.F. Long, also by Joekerr), published by Graphic Postcard Co., New York.

United States, by B.F. Long (Axis Series by B.F. Long, also by Joekerr), published by Graphic Postcard Co., New York.

United States, by B.F. Long (Axis Series by B.F. Long, also by Joekerr), published by Graphic Postcard Co., New York.

United States, published by Graphic Postcard Co., New York City.

Scatological anti-Axis propaganda postcards were common in the United States during World War II. They were not necessarily crude or obscene, however, and differ significantly from ordinary lavatory drawing. Prior to the war, no artist would dream of turning out scatology of this type for general consumption, but "unmentionable" acts directed at the Axis leaders were not only accepted, they were welcomed. The card above, titled "Heil Hitler!" shows a dog urinating in Hitler's mouth in preference to a fire hydrant. The dog is nearly a dead ringer for Spot, the irrepressible mutt of the *Dick and Jane* primary grade readers. Hitler closely resembles one of the Three Stooges, who made farcical movies. The fire hydrant appears to be taken from the Little Golden Books, a series of benign adventures for children. Hence, the effect is not threatening or subversive, but comic and innocent.

The glossy black and white postcard above, numbered 70 in the Axis Series and copyrighted HNA, was produced by the Graphic Postcard Co. of New York City; 27 different cards have been identified but some of the same images contain different numbers. Many have survived in pristine condition because numerous senders enclosed them in an outside envelope before mailing, suggesting they felt awkward dealing with the subject matter on the cards.

United States, published by American Offset Printing, Los Angeles.

Anti-Axis postcard publishers such as the American Offset Printing of Los Angeles frequently used wordplay to get their message across. Here the Axis powers of Germany, Italy, and Japan (the Berlin-Rome-Tokyo Axis) were cleverly tied in with the word for the wood-cutting tools axes, which are popularly associated with crude but violent murder and planted in the heads of Hitler, Mussy (Mussolini), and Hirohito. Italy's Benito Mussolini first coined the term Axis on October 25, 1936, referring to a Rome-Berlin Axis after signing an agreement of diplomatic cooperation with Hitler "in the interests of peace and reconstruction" and "to defend the great institutions of Europe." Then on September 27, 1940, Japan, along with Italy and Germany, signed a ten-year military-economic alliance in Berlin, creating a totalitarian, three-dimensional Axis.

No one captured life at the front better than Bill Mauldin who was a front line soldier himself. Enlisting at age 17 and awarded a Purple Heart, Mauldin created "Up Front," first rejected by *Yank* magazine for showing too much of the dirty side of an ugly war through the disheveled principle characters Willie and Joe. The 45th Division newspaper accepted "Up Front" and Mauldin's career escalated rapidly, as his work became immensely popular with the front line troops he represented so well. What he "exposed" and what made him so popular with the troops was not the dirt and horror of war, but, as underscored nicely in this postcard, the bogus good news of the official propaganda so characteristic of all officialdom, press agents, and advertising. The only cartoon trooper in the same league as Willie and Joe was the hapless Sad Sack, whose main enemies seemed to be blowhard sergeants and diabolical lieutenants.

"*Fresh, spirited American troops, flushed with victory, are bringing in thousands of hungry, ragged, battle-weary prisoners.*" (NEWS ITEM)

United States, by Bill Mauldin.

Pearl Harbor Navy Yard employees have a laugh at an ex-dictator. This is a picture of a two color poster produced within the yard.

United States, published by Pearl Harbor Navy Yard, after the fall of Mussolini.

Benito Mussolini was the first of the Axis leaders to fall, captured by Italian partisans April 27, 1945, and executed by firing squad the next day, along with his mistress Clara Petacci. Their bodies were strung up by their feet in front of a Milan gasoline station. Utilizing a baseball theme, employees at the Pearl Harbor Navy Yard produced a two-color poster as well as postcards showing Mussolini swinging and missing, the first Axis dictator to strike out while the scoreboard proclaims "1 Down, 2 To Go." In Allied propaganda, Mussolini was nearly always depicted as Hitler's stooge, a dunce who did whatever the German leader wanted, or as an incompetent thug. Before gaining power, in fact, Hitler copied many of Mussolini's ideas, such as using radio and public speeches to manipulate public opinion and the strong arm tactics of his own private army. Hitler's brown shirts were copied directly from Mussolini's black shirts and Mussolini was forming Italian youth brigades long before Hitler's "Jungvolk" movement. Mussolini's fantasies of a second Roman Empire ultimately made the Italian leader subservient to Hitler and before the end he was little more than a lackey.

This advertising postcard for the Interstate Theatres movie chain in Texas was published by Jimmie Allard on V-E (Victory in Europe) Day, May 8, 1945, with the welcome news, "Dear Interstater - Two Down and One to Go." Using downed bowling pins to represent Mussolini and Hitler, the two Axis powers already defeated, a pin representing Hirohito remains precariously standing. (On August 15, 1945, three months and a week after Germany's unconditional surrender, Japan surrendered unconditionally.) In the background is a GI sending a bowling ball straight for the Japanese Emperor. The spectators are also service personnel. It was common for such businesses as movie theaters and bowling lanes to provide servicemen and women with free admission as their "contribution" to the war effort. The entertainment was a welcome respite from camp life and proved to be a morale booster. It was also good advertising and a cheap way of encouraging consumer habits: bowling flourished in the postwar era.

United States, published by Interstate Theatres, Texas, 1945.

"A Close Shave for Three Bad Boys" features an unnamed GI pretending to shave the Axis leaders painted on three bombs (left to right: Tojo, Hitler, Mussolini). Imaginative artwork on bombs and shells became standard procedure during World War II as caricatures and messages, many obscene, were painted on them before they were used against the Axis. It was psychologically uplifting for these artists, many of whom never saw front line duty. Though genuine folk art, few originals remain, for obvious reasons, though some postcard renditions do endure. Postcards from World War I depict artillery shells similarly addressed. One pictured in John Laffin's *World War I in Postcards* is titled "A Present for the Kaiser" and shows a monster shell addressed, "To Willie with Compliments."

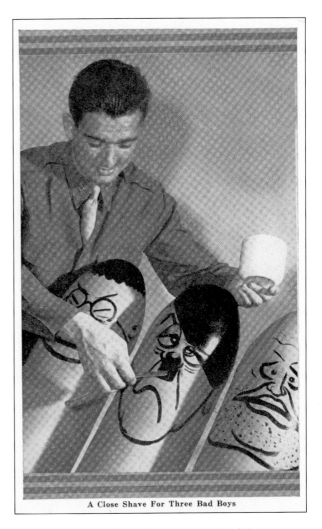

A Close Shave For Three Bad Boys

United States, published by Graycraft Card Co., Danville, VA.

Without question, the United States turned out more scatological propaganda humor than all the other warring nations combined. There's nothing very subtle about the card below entitled "Uncle Sam's Peace Terms" as it shows Tojo, Hitler, and Mussolini lined up behind Uncle Sam, ready to kiss his ass. Most of these cards leave little to the imagination, but brought the Axis leaders down to the lowest level possible and provoked hearty laughs. Since Hitler and Mussolini were infamous for long and ranting speeches, to have them perform the gesture of submission from a soapbox is apt, though the ridiculous caricatures of the Axis trio makes the card more comical than obscene. Most cards of this type were not sent through the mail, as many people were afraid they would not be delivered because of their content. Such cards would be passed among trusted friends and treated in much the same manner as truly pornographic material. This cartoon is mild by today's standards, but 50 years ago it was considered extremely risqué.

United States, a number of similar cards, with the same theme but different details, have been examined and none have the name of the publisher listed.

United States, published by L.L. Cook Co., Milwaukee, WI.

It was not the least bit unusual for postcard publishers to borrow ideas from one another as they cranked out anti-Axis propaganda. The card above was part of an anti-Axis set published by the L.L. Cook Co. of Milwaukee, which specialized in photo postcards. Entitled "Der Phewrer," a play on the German word Fuerher (leader), it is card #27 in L.L. Cook's vast array of anti-Axis cards. Hitler's head is inside the toilet hollering "Benito" (Mussolini,) implausibly beseeching the Italian leader for help. The card on the right, by Charles J. Herbert of Traverse City, Michigan, uses the same theme but has Hitler facing in the opposite direction. Both use the explicit idea that Hitler, as fecal matter, has a decidedly bad odor, another example of scatological humor employed by many American postcard manufacturers. The scatology is socially redeemed by the humor: Mussolini's military incompetence was so vast that his talents must lie more in the area of the commode bowl.

United States, by Charles J. Herbert, published by Charles J. Herbert, Traverse City, MI.

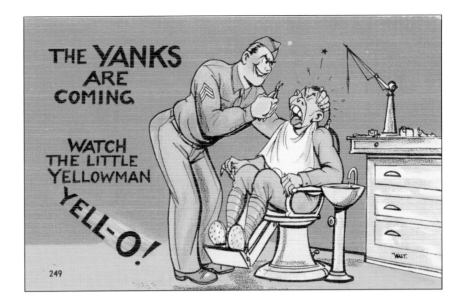

United States, by Walt Munson, published by Colour Picture Publications, Cambridge, MA.

Racial stereotyping, politically incorrect in peacetime but a readily accepted propaganda tool during wars, depicted the Japanese as small, weak-eyed, bucktoothed, and yellow. Artist Walt Munson's double entendre on yellow and Yanks (Americans) cleverly combines humor and hate. Yellow not only refers to Japanese skin pigment but to the cowardly way Pearl Harbor was attacked (early on a Sunday morning when most Americans in Hawaii were asleep or, for propaganda purposes, in church). Borrowing from George M. Cohan's World War I anthem, "The Yanks Are Coming," Munson shows the "little yellow man" turning to Jell-O, here as "Yell-O," as Dr. Sgt. Yank, adorned with a sadistic grin, prepares to teach his inferior adversary a lesson he'll never forget. (Yanking out his buckteeth without anesthetic for starters.) American hatred against Japan was real, enhanced by the sneak attack on Pearl Harbor and by true stories of atrocities against American POWs. Because the initial stages of the war went badly for the United States, early propaganda postcards like this nurtured the hatred and enabled Americans to feel superior to an enemy that held the upper hand. Interestingly, the Japanese soldier in this particular postcard is as big as his GI counterpart, which is unusual.

Private Breger was the mischievous alter ego of cartoonist Dave Breger, who parlayed his army experiences into a highly successful comic strip carried in hundreds of newspapers by King Features as well as the military daily *Stars and Stripes* where it originated. Another Breger comic strip character, G.I. (Government Issue) Joe Ranger became so popular the term G.I. Joe became synonymous with American troops everywhere. G.I. Joe made his debut in *Yank* magazine in 1942 and the term has lived on ever since. In more recent years, G.I. Joe has been a children's action figure, a television cartoon, and the scourge of international terrorism. This card showing Pvt. Breger with a mischievous look on his face while flying a kite carrying the message "Phooey on the Fuerher," captures the essence of Dave Breger's humor.

United States, by Dave Breger, published by Graycraft Card Co., Danville, VA.

The Women's Army Corps, established in May 1942 under the direction of Col. Oveta Culp, grew to a wartime peak of 99,000 members by April 1945. Their contribution to the war effort was monumental; WACs took over jobs normally held by men who were thus freed for combat duty. The postcard entitled "We're Giving 'Em a Big WAC" shows a snappy and attractive WAC smashing a befuddled, childish Hitler on the head with a rolling pin. Created to evoke a hearty laugh, it was distributed by the Asheville, North Carolina Postcard Co., both to glamorize the Women's Army Corps and acknowledge their contribution to the war effort. Though they were prohibited from combat duty, female service personnel helped both to defeat the Axis and destroy stereotypes about a woman's "proper place." Nor were women restricted to army duty. The Women's Naval Service, Women Accepted for Volunteer Service (W.A.V.E.S.) was formed in July 1943. Headed by Captain Mildred McAfee, it reached a wartime peak of 90,000 in July 1945. Some of the most heroic volunteers, Women Air Force Service Pilots (W.A.S.E.) ferried planes across the Atlantic and reached a strength of 916 under the direction of Jacqueline Cochran, a well-known aviation pioneer.

United States, by Max Halverson, published by Beals, Des Moines, IA, distributed by Asheville Postcard Co., NC.

United States, by P. Snyder, published by Gulfport Printing Co., MS, mailed September 1943.

Support units that never fire a shot in anger play a pivotal role in the success of any warring nation's armed forces. Airplane mechanics were among the foremost contributors to the war effort as they kept allied fighters and bombers functioning properly on an around-the-clock basis. Artist P. Snyder salutes them in a postcard produced by the Gulfport Printing Co. in Mississippi, which was sold at Kessler Field in Biloxi and Gulfport Field, where aircraft mechanics were trained. This postcard shows the odious and odorous trio: Tojo as a snake, Hitler as a rat, and Mussolini as a bug, with tails held by a wrench-wielding mechanic, a clothespin on his nose and a satisfied look on his face. Waxing poetic, he says, "The Axis stirs up quite a stench in seeking domination, but here I am, and here's my wrench to bring extermination."

Postcards printed on a thin piece of wood are a rare novelty to begin with, and one with an anti-Hitler message is extremely hard to find. This clever unsigned card produced by Dixie Novelty Co. in Asheville, North Carolina, shows two rats, one with a gun pointed to his head saying to the other, "Don't stop me. I just heard Hitler is a rat." Referring to Axis leaders as such lowly-regarded animals as rats, skunks, and snakes was standard procedure with World War II propaganda artists and numerous caricatures of Hitler, Goering, and Tojo picture them with monkey or rat tails. By portraying the enemy as animals, it not only evoked images of their bestiality, it provided a sense of superiority. The comic rodents here belong to the same family as the comic book and cartoon mice Tom and Jerry, and are an example of how readily

United States, published by Dixie Novelty Co., Asheville, NC, value $25-$50.

American popular culture is turned to propaganda use, generally with a humorous twist. Other postcards of the war period were printed or drawn on a number of surfaces including leather and birch bark.

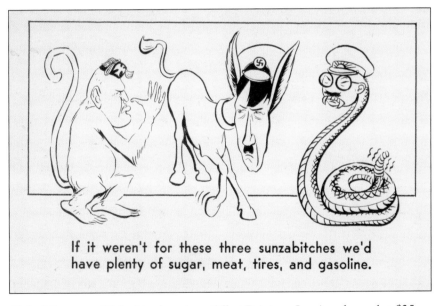

United States, published by American Offset Printers, Los Angeles, value $25-$50.

During World War II the civilian population of the United States was extremely fortunate in that they were never faced with the more horrific aspects of war such as bombing and artillery attacks to which those in Europe and Asia were exposed. However, their normal lives were greatly affected by shortages of everyday goods taken for granted prior to the war. This postcard produced by American Offset Printers in Los Angeles points out four of the most sorely missed items. Showing Mussolini as a monkey thumbing his nose at Hitler, Hitler as a jackass, and Hirohito as a snake, the risqué caption reads, "If it weren't for these three sunzabitches we'd have plenty of sugar, meat, tires and gasoline." Before the war, no postcard publisher would dare have used the word "sunzabitches" on a card to be sent through the mail. Directing this language at the hated enemies made it acceptable.

Gasoline rationing went into effect for the first time in 17 states on May 18, 1942, as people with non-essential vehicles were only allowed three gallons per week. Gasoline was rationed nationwide on December 1, 1942. That meant long distance driving vacations were a thing of the past. In addition to the four items on the postcard, butter, coffee, most canned and frozen foods, and shoes were all rationed at one time or another. But despite these inconveniences, America's civilian population was spared the devastation that wracked the rest of the world.

Propaganda Postcards of World War II - The Allies

No. 513. The End of a Busy Day.

IF THIS WERE HITLER!

WHAT WOULD YOU DO CHUMS?

De groene politiebeulen.

Het bekende aanplakbiljet.

HELLEP! HELP!

DUITSCHLAND WINT OP ALLE FRONT Pagina's

IT WILL BE A FAR FAR BETTER WORLD SOON DEAR !

This Canadian postcard shows Hitler as a chained gorilla becoming enraged at the sound of "There'll Always Be an England," one of World War II's most popular songs. The stamped date, November 12, 1941 - some 14 months after the end of the Battle of Britain - indicates the importance of propaganda myth for home consumption. No longer did Britain stand alone. The bulk of the German armed forces and all Hitler's attention were directed to the war in Russia, where the critical battle of Stalingrad was about to begin. To the British, however, the fact that the putative Operation Sea Lion (the Nazi invasion of the home islands) didn't take place remained the war's most heroic triumph.

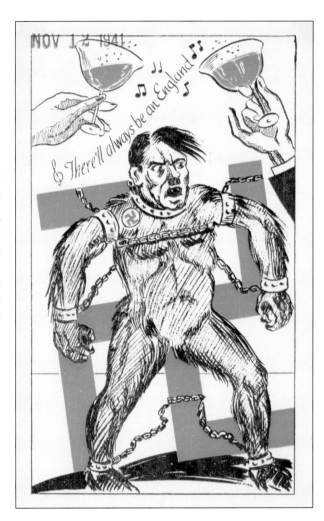

Canada, 1941, value $25-$50.

Canada, by Wilf Long, published by Canadian Photogelatine Engraving Co., Ottawa, value $25-$50.

This postcard by Canadian artist Wilf Long puts World War II in perspective. Hitler was indeed "Sittin' Pretty for 'A Time'" but there was a time bomb under him fused by the Allies growing strength spearheaded by America's entry into the war on December 8, 1941, one day after Japan's attack on Pearl Harbor. However, the United States did not declare war on Germany. It was the other way around: Germany and Italy declared war on the United States on December 11, four days after Pearl Harbor. Caught up in the euphoria of the moment and limited by his prejudices, Hitler felt the United States was a racial mongrel whose lack of Aryan virtues had been expressed by Japan's surprise attack. It was a monumental miscalculation. The influx of American troops in addition to its mammoth war production capabilities created the war machine that ultimately destroyed the Axis.

Canada, published by Photogelatine Engraving Co., Ottawa.

Before World War II many homes throughout the world did not have indoor plumbing and chamber pots were a fact of ordinary life. It was only natural that the faces of the Axis leaders would adorn these pots on many propaganda postcards. This highly unusual Canadian card shows three identifiable potty-heads and one chamber pot bearing only swastikas, with a lamenting message from Hitler: "That 'wop' Benito, Hirohito and me. We make up the Holy Three. But who's the stranger, I cannot guess. May be that scum Rudolph Hess. Destroy him or he'll drive me bugs. He'll think he's one of us Thunder Mugs." At one time Hess was Hitler's designated successor but he lost favor with the Fuehrer. Then on May 10, 1941, Hess mysteriously took off for England in a borrowed plane and parachuted out over Scotland where a farmer captured him with a pitchfork. Hess claimed his mission was to meet with the Duke of Hamilton whom he had met at the 1936 Olympic Games and who could put him in touch with British leaders in hopes of signing a separate peace with Great Britain, allowing Germany to attack Russia with impunity. Hitler was furious and claimed Hess was mentally deranged. Hess was imprisoned and remained so until he died at Spandau Prison in 1987 at the age of 91. His mission was one of the most bizarre of World War II and will probably never be fully understood.

Bonzo, the lovable pudgy puppy created by artist George Studdy in 1922, was every bit as popular in England as Walt Disney's Mickey Mouse and Donald Duck were in the United States a decade later. When World War II began, Bonzo, like everyone else in England, rallied behind the war effort. In this delightful comic postcard published by Valentine & Sons, Ltd. in 1939, Studdy borrows the famous Winston Churchill quote regarding a far better world without Hitler, while having Bonzo knock Hitler off the face of the earth with a solid punch in the nose. Bonzo first appeared in *Sketch* magazine in 1922 and became such a popular merchandising tool he was featured in advertisements, books, films, and on toys, pottery, and postcards to mention only a few. Studdy, born in Devonshire in 1878, lived long enough to see Great Britain and Bonzo triumph over Hitler and the Axis powers. He died in 1948, leaving behind a legacy of creating one of the most popular comic characters in history. Everyone related to Bonzo because he was mischievous without being mean and came to personify every man as he faced life's trials and tribulations with a marvelous sense of humor. Fifty years after his creator's death, Bonzo postcards and other items are highly sought after collectibles.

Britain, by George Studdy, published by Valentine & Sons, Ltd., 1939, value $50 and up.

Sans lui le monde serait bien meilleur.

IT WILL BE A FAR FAR BETTER WORLD SOON DEAR !

Britain, by Donald McGill, National Series. Note: Card showing Kaiser was by an unknown artist who copied the McGill classic.

Donald McGill was Great Britain's all-time most prolific post-card artist, with more than 10,000 different designs during his long career. Many were risqué seaside comics but he contributed to the propaganda effort during both World Wars. His World War I anti-Kaiser comic titled "Swat that Fly" became so popular that other artists copied the idea with only the slightest variation: such as this example by an anonymous artist. When World War II broke out 21 years later, Hitler replaced the Kaiser as public enemy #1. Dusting off his World War I classic, McGill substituted Hitler's face for that of the Kaiser with equally good result. When World War II ended, McGill went back to his saucy seaside cartoons that produced hearty laughs for generations of British vacationers. McGill died in 1962 at the age 87. Because of his longevity and productivity, Donald McGill is the perfect artist to serve as the transition from World War I to World War II. Although the type of war was totally different, propaganda art was surprisingly similar.

Britain, by Donald McGill, published by New Donald McGill Comics, value $25-$50.

GERMAN RADIO 18 JULY 1941

"The Russians have thrown in their last reserves."

GERMAN RADIO 8 DAYS LATER!

"The Russians have shown themselves able time and again to bring up fresh units."

Britain, published by British Ministry of Information (MOI), value $25-$50.

Without question the British dual image cards from Brendan Bracken's Ministry of Information were as effective as any propaganda postcards produced by anyone during World War II. So effective, in fact, they appeared in many languages for distribution throughout the world. The idea was simplicity itself and brilliant in its execution. Quotations from actual German broadcasts and the date appear on the top panel with caricatures of Hitler and other Nazi leaders. The bottom panel shows what actually happened, along with the date it occurred.

By casting aspersions on the veracity of all German propaganda broadcasts, the postcards minimized their effectiveness. People began trusting British propaganda as the repository of the real truth. The British government produced hundreds of different postcards of this type and here are two of the better examples.

The first card shows Hitler and two of his generals marching triumphantly while German radio on July 18, 1941, proclaims, "The Russians have thrown in their last reserves." The bottom panel shows Hitler and his generals running for their lives being chased by Russian tanks and planes. Just eight days later, German radio says, "The Russians have shown themselves able time and again to bring up fresh units." Time and again during the war, Russia's ability to call in fresh troops turned defeat into victory. The second actually quotes a passage from Hitler's autobiography, *Mein Kampf.* "The great masses of the people are more easily victimised (sic) by a large than a small lie." Turning the quote around, the postcard states, "But the big lie cannot stand up to the truth" and shows people listening to "Truthful BBC News" while Goebbels is quoted from an August 15, 1941, broadcast saying, "We introduce the death penalty for listening to the BBC." Two more of these outstanding cards are shown in the Neutral section under Portugal, one of the nations flooded with them.

Britain, published by British Ministry of Information (MOI), value $25-$50.

Hitler's autobiography, *Mein Kampf* (My Struggle), written while he was serving a prison sentence during the 1920s, was required reading in Nazi Germany when Hitler came to power in 1932. Leave it to the British to have fun with the book's title and Hitler at the same time. The green tone card by Star Press in Liverpool titled appropriately "Me In Kamp," shows Hitler dressed in women's clothes pulling up his stockings while Herman Goering peeks through an opening in his tent. The added hilarious nuance shows a Dachshund, the dog most associated with Germany, reading *Mein Kampf* with a disgusted look on his face. Hitler's hatred of the Jews was clearly evident in the book and served as a warning of the unspeakable acts he would commit against them in the future.

Britain, published by Star Press, Liverpool, value $25-$50.

Britain, by Fougasse, published by Vase Press Ltd., Throxton and London, value $25-$50.

Artist Cyril Kenneth Bird (1887-1965), using the nom de plume Fougasse (a small explosive), made humor an integral part of his propaganda art. A longtime art editor for the British humor magazine *Punch*, Fougasse donated his services to produce eight posters dealing with the subject "Careless talk costs lives." Bringing a smile as well as making a serious point, the posters made Britons aware that talk pertaining to the war could indeed cost the lives of their loved ones, if overheard by the wrong people. Using Hitler and Goering as the eavesdroppers, the playful posters were also produced as postcards and were extremely effective. Another cartoon in the series shows a man in a red British phone booth surrounded by no less than a dozen Hitlers saying, "But for Heaven's sake, don't say I told you!"

The fact that all or nearly all German spies were either under British "control" and serving as double agents or in custody was not known to the public or the artist. The frequently stated message involved people in the war effort and imposed military discipline in a manner that had widespread approval.

The "careless talk" posters and postcards live on half a century later along with other Fougasse themes (waste the food and help the Hun) as modern reproductions that are on sale at the Imperial War Museum in London and elsewhere. To many Britons, the bright Fougasse images will forever be associated with the dreary home front and the blitz.

"I THOUGHT THEY SAID YOU WAS DEAD!"

Britain, by Akki.

The British have always been able to rely on their marvelous sense of humor to make the best of a bad situation. They had little else to fall back on after France's capitulation on June 20, 1940, and Great Britain stood alone against Hitler and his Nazi legions. Despite stories to the contrary, Hitler was an artist of considerable talent, with his landscapes being particularly good. But with little else to cheer about early in the war, the British and later the Americans took great delight in depicting Hitler as a house painter or paper hanger and these two cards illustrate that. The first, by Akki, shows a diminutive Hitler look-alike with brush and paint bucket in hand, walking between three skeptical Britons. The back of the card carries an encouraging message from King George VI: "Help to make the world a better place and life a worthier thing." Messages like this from the King and Prime Minister, Winston Churchill, frequently adorned the back of wartime propaganda postcards. Rumors of Hitler's death occurred frequently during the war. An unsuccessful attempt on his life actually occurred in 1944, but he received only minor injuries.

The other postcard, produced by Bamforth, pokes fun at the Hitler family's original name of Schickelgruber, changed by his father many years before. The wheelbarrow carries wallpaper samples in addition to the paint and brush and is marked "Mr. Schickelgruber, Painter & Decorator."

Britian, published by Bamforth.

David Low, a left-leaning political cartoonist for Lord Beaverbrook's *Evening Standard*, who was born in New Zealand, emerged as Great Britain's most famous political cartoonist before World War II. Prior to the war, he was decidedly pro-Soviet and an admirer of Joseph Stalin and so strongly anti-Hitler and anti-Fascist that his works were immediately banned in Germany. Imagine his shock and chagrin when Russia and Germany signed a non-aggression pact in September 1939 and promptly divided Poland between them. This Low cartoon, probably his most frequently published, appeared on September 20, 1939, and shows Hitler and Stalin curtsying over the dead body of Poland. "The scum of the earth, I believe," Hitler exclaims with a courtly bow, while Stalin replies,

Britain, by David Low, as a cartoon for the London Evening Standard, 1939.

"The bloody assassin of the workers, I presume?" The brilliance of the art lies not so much in Low's astonishment at such an unholy alliance, but at its brazen cynicism reflected by the dictators' ballroom manners as they pretend years of vituperative rhetoric was polite and complimentary discourse. Like many of the better British World War II cartoons, this Low classic was reproduced as a postcard in Portugal.

Britain, published by Dufay-Chromex, Ltd., Elstree, Hurts, value $50 and up.

Hold-to-light novelty postcards have long been popular among collectors and are extremely rare when they are used to vilify Hitler. A hold-to-light is a card that changes dramatically when held to the light. The use of light-emitting perforations and translucent tissue paper creates these illusions as light comes through the back of the card. This example, published by Dufay-Chromex Ltd. in Elstree, England, shows Hitler holding a copy of *Mein Kampf* in his raised right hand. It contains the following verse: "The man of froth once wrote a book and called the tripe *Mein Kampf*. But now we know he named it wrong, it should have been *Mein Ramp*." In the lower right hand corner the verse reads, "To see the doom of this Nazi spark, hold this card to the light and look in the dark." When held to the light in a darkened room, Hitler becomes a skeleton with flames surrounding him. Ironically, the card proved prophetic, since Hitler committed suicide and then had his body burned. But as the artist could not have predicted the literal flaming end of his mortal remains, it's likely the allusion is to Hitler's honored residence in Hell.

Britain.

Whereas American propaganda postcards were often scatological, British propaganda for the most part relied on the tongue-in-cheek approach. These particular examples are about as close as the British came to lavatory humor. The first, titled "Homeward Bound," shows Hitler giving the Nazi salute while his planes are headed right for the toilet. The German Luftwaffe's inability to win the Battle of Britain during the summer and early autumn of 1940 inspired flights of eloquent Churchillian rhetoric and propaganda myths that endured for generations. It also cost Germany an estimated 2,698 airplanes and preserved Britain as the base from which a second front was launched nearly four years later. The second card shows an obviously distressed Hitler racing to the W.C. (water closet), hoping to get there in time.

Britain.

98

"I'm Dreaming of a White Christmas" was Irving Berlin's classic Christmas song, immortalized by Bing Crosby in the 1942 Paramount motion picture *Holiday Inn*. The talented British comic artist Laurie Taylor used this theme by showing a shivering dejected Hitler sitting forlornly in the snow in this propaganda offering from the venerable Tuck and Sons Ltd. It captured the plight of the German army outside Moscow, Leningrad, and Stalingrad in 1942, as the Russian winter took its toll on what initially British and German officialdom alike thought would be an easy Nazi victory. Unprepared for the frigid cold, many German troops, wearing summer clothing, froze to death; tanks, trucks, planes, and guns failed to function because of the below-zero temperatures. Napoleon's advance a century before was stymied by the Russian winter within sight of Moscow and Hitler suffered the same fate.

Britain, by Laurie Taylor, published by Tuck and Sons Ltd., 1943, value $50 and up.

This postcard is rather sophisticated, as much of the British postcard humor of the World War II period tended to be a lot like the seaside postcards, featuring ladies with big bottoms and men with big bellies. A salesman with an immense stomach says, "I'm telling you! If Hitler wants any more territory he can have mine," and in another by Arnold Taylor, famous for his seaside ladies with enormous posteriors, we have an enormous male bum pointed at the viewer with the question, "If this were Hitler! What would you do chums?"

Britain, by Arnold Taylor, published by Tuck and Sons Ltd., 1943.

VOILA LE TRUC POUR DEVENIR CHAMPION!
DAT IS DE MANIER OM KAMPIOEN TE WORDEN!
THAT'S THE THING TO BECOME A CHAMPION!

Belgium, pre-invasion.

On April 10, 1940, Belgium rejected Allied "Preventive Aid," declaring her neutrality in the hope she could remain out of World War II, which by this time had been underway for seven months. This reluctance was understandable, since most of World War I was fought on her soil. Using a pretext of "irrefutable evidence" that the Allies were about to attack Germany through Belgium, the Netherlands, and Luxembourg, the Nazis had invaded the three lowland countries on May 10. It was a successful feint to hold the French army in place while enveloping it in a daring offensive through the Ardennes. Less than three weeks later, on May 28, King Leopold surrendered unconditionally despite pleas from his ministers that he should continue the fight by forming a government in exile in London, instead choosing to remain in seclusion at a quiet castle near Brussels for the remainder of the war. France, in the meantime, had collapsed as a military power.

This cute Belgian drawing is one of the few anti-Hitler post-cards, albeit a mild one, produced during the brief period Belgium was in the war. It shows a youngster practicing on a punching bag adorned with Hitler's face. The three-language caption, French, Walloon (Flemish), and English says, "That's the thing to become a champion." Germany, however, had no intention of fighting another unsuccessful draw, as in 1914-18, and her off-road work and rope skipping produced a first-round knock out. The Belgian army had all the punch of the cute kid in the drawing when it came to stopping the Nazis.

The Belgians obviously felt there was safety in numbers as the second card suggests Hitler would be no match for the French, British, and Belgian Allies. Generally, with three against one, the odds are definitely in your favor. However, Belgian resistance against Hitler's powerful war machine was about as feeble as what would be offered by the three children shown on the card. It was child's play for Hitler's army to make quick work of Allied forces in Belgium. With almost childlike innocence, the unnamed artist treats war as a child's game, when in reality it was a brutal experience for all those affected by it. This postcard was produced during the three weeks Belgium was involved in the war. Because of its brevity as a combatant, images like this produced before Belgium's capitulation are extremely hard to find.

Belgium, pre-invasion.

WHAT CAN HITLER DO AGAINST THREE.

While many South American countries remained neutral during World War II, Brazil was outspoken in opposing Axis tyranny. On January 29, 1942, only seven weeks after Japan attacked Pearl Harbor, Brazil broke off diplomatic relations with the Axis powers and then declared war on August 22, 1942. This clever Brazilian postcard has the perfect recipe for a Merry Christmas and Happy New Year in 1943. The New Year's Baby is choking Hitler, holding Hirohito by his feet, and stomping on Mussolini. In the Brazilian national colors of blue, yellow, and green, it emphasizes Brazil's commitment on the propaganda as well as the military front.

Orphaned by a Japanese bombing attack on Shanghai, Ping Mei, "one of 30 million children left motherless, fatherless, homeless by four years of merciless war," miraculously survived and served as the sad and pathetic poster child, whose image, amid the devastation of war, was used to raise money for United China Relief, Inc., 1790 Broadway, New York. The graphic scene on this postcard was captured on newsreels shown in movie theaters throughout the world, emphasizing war's horrific toll on innocents like Ping Mei in China and elsewhere.

Though statistics in wartime are even more suspect than is usually the case, no reliable figures for casualties and refugees in China exist. Due in part to the sponsorship of such public figures as Henry Luce (the proprietor of Time, Inc.) and Mme. Chaing Kai-Shek (the Wellesley educated wife of the Generalissimo), the Chinese were given different stereotypes in propaganda from those assigned to the Japanese. Typically, they were heroic, noble, and long-suffering victims, capable of becoming oriental Christians until the Communists gained power in 1949, when they became indistinguishable from the wartime Japanese.

Brazil, by A. Turista, Recife, 1942, value $50 and up.

United States, published by United China Relief, New York.

The Czech people were the first, other than the Germans themselves, to fall under the yoke of Nazi tyranny. After the British-French Appeasement at Munich, German troops marched into the Sudetenland on October 1, 1938. The dismemberment of Czechoslovakia was completed on March 14, 1939, when Germany took control of the rest of the country. However, the idea of freedom did not die, especially with groups such as the Czech-American National Alliance, who issued a series of postcards from their Chicago headquarters showing a male shackled to two swastika-laden and serpent-guarded pillars with his distraught family close by. The message below states, "Join in our fight to free Czechoslovakia in free Europe! For lasting peace and freedom! For safety of all countries of the world from aggression and lawlessness." This postcard was mailed to a family in Milwaukee on September 22, 1939, only three weeks after World War II officially began following Germany's invasion of Poland.

United States, by Czech-American National Alliance, published by Colorprinting Co., Chicago, mailed September 1939, value $25-$50.

Czechoslovakia, by Otto Usak, value $25-$50.

In 1938 Czechoslovakia was preparing to celebrate its 20th anniversary, as this first postcard by Otto Usak indicates. Their celebration was short lived, however, as the young nation was decimated when Hitler was able to gain control of the Sudetenland, the heart of the Czech Republic, without firing a shot. This was part of the Munich Agreement worked out by Hitler, Italy's Benito Mussolini, France's Edouard Daladier, and Neville Chamberlain of Great Britain. It was a blatant case of peace through dishonor. President Eduard Benes of Czechoslovakia was conspicuous by his absence. He resigned in disgust a week after the Munich Agreement was reached. However, on July 23, 1940, a provisional government of Czechoslovakia was established in London with Dr. Benes as President and Mgr Stramek as Vice President. Nearly a year later, on July 18, 1941, Great Britain formally recognized the Benes government as the legal provisional government. It was standard procedure for the countries occupied by Germany to form governments in exile in London. Although the military forces of these nations were small, they fought ardently under Allied command. The second postcard was published by the Czechoslovak army and air force in Great Britain and features a special cancel to commemorate Dr. Benes' 60th birthday in 1944.

Britain, published by Czechoslovak army and air force, 1944.

There's a real touch of irony to this postcard showing Lady Czechoslovakia on her knees thanking the Russian soldier for liberating her country from the Nazi oppressors. Note the Soviet soldier is trampling on the Nazi flag while flag-waving Czechs cheer in the background. In reality, Czechoslovakia was trading one oppressor for another. However, in fairness, the Czechs fared better than most nations under Communist rule until she gained her complete freedom in the "Velvet Revolution" of 1989. The date on this postcard is May 9, 1945, when Germany officially surrendered. But fighting was still going on in a pocket east of the Czech capitol of Prague two days later. On May 11, Field Marshall Ferdinand Schoerner, in command of German Army Group, Center, surrendered to the Russians. Now indeed the war in Europe was over.

Czechoslovakia, 1945, value $25-$50.

This fabulous postcard titled "La Nouvelle Danse, l'europa Walk Pax" (The New Dance: The Europe Peace Walk) shows the four signers of the Munich Pact (September 29, 1938) dancing for joy over what they had accomplished. From left to right are Great Britain's Neville Chamberlain, Germany's Adolph Hitler, Italy's Benito Mussolini, and France's Edouard Daladier. The pact allowed Germany to take over the Sudetenland in Czechoslovakia, promising to seek no further territory. England and France "guaranteed" the new Czech boundaries. Neither commitment was honored. Conspicuous by his absence is Czechoslovakia's President Eduard Benes, who resigned in protest less than a week later. After the Munich Pact was signed, Chamberlain proudly proclaimed "Peace in our time" but subsequent events proved it was appeasement at its worst. Hitler concluded that Britain and France wouldn't honor their subsequent pledge to fight on behalf of "Polish integrity." Less than a year after Munich, "Peace in our time" became World War II. A French postcard on which men and women cannot be distinguished is most certainly not complimenting any of those pictured.

Ironically, one of the neatest bits of World War II propaganda occurred when Hitler was shown dancing a "victory jig" on the occasion of the French surrender in June 1940. The world was stunned to see this ridiculous wartime newsreel shot, which helped prove his madness. The truth came out in 1958 when British documentary filmmaker John Grierson told the *London Sunday Dispatch* that he had taken a film of Hitler and through tricky cutting, freezing, and editing, had created the dance that never took place.

France, by A. Migret, Menton, value $50 and up.

No. 513. THE END OF A BUSY DAY.

Egypt, by Saroukhan, published by Eastern Publishing Co.,
Cairo, value $25-$50.

The enterprising Egyptian postcard artist Saroukhan took advantage of Cairo's location as a rest and relaxation center for British and other Allied troops engaged in the desert war. Cairo was a delightful oasis for the Desert Rats who often faced terrible conditions as they battled German General Erwin Rommel's army for command of North Africa. Cairo offered many attractions including beautiful women and well-stocked bars with names such as Spitfire and Churchill's that provided a brief respite from the war. The famous Shepheards Hotel was the command center for the staff of General Headquarters Middle East where Allied operations in that area were planned. Since the postcards sold to the soldiers had to be approved by British censors, Saroukhan made certain they were decidedly pro-British in content as well as humorous. Surprisingly, many luxury items unavailable in England because of the war were readily available in the Cairo stores, so it was a shopping paradise as well. With skilled pen, Saroukhan depicted all aspects of life in and around Cairo during this period, but also made a point of showing British success on the battlefield against German and Italian forces; thus marketing his product extremely well as evidenced by these three examples.

No. 514. An Unexpected Visitor.

Egypt, by Saroukhan, published by Eastern Publishing Co., Cairo, value $25-$50.

No. 516. Fireworks.

Egypt, by Saroukhan, published by Eastern Publishing Co., Cairo, value $25-$50.

France, by P. Remy, value $25-$50.

After mortal enemies Adolph Hitler and Joseph Stalin signed a non-aggression pact on August 23, 1939, only a week before Germany invaded Poland, a skeptical world and French artist P. Remy wondered how long such an unlikely alliance could last. Remy's prophetic caption, "They are waiting for the other to turn his back," under the scene of Hitler and Stalin watching each other with poised daggers, became reality on June 22, 1941, when Hitler struck the first blow by invading Russia. Though repeatedly warned of the impending attack, Stalin refused to admit he had met his match in deceitful cynicism. Compared to David Low's cartoon on the same occasion, Remy's work is effective but obvious.

A postcard depicting Hitler's severed head steaming in a cooking pot with the caption, "Coming with Pig," underscores the degree to which the French naively regarded themselves and the war. The comic style of cartoonist Pierre Ugrere depicts a smiling soldier wearing the bright blue of the Poilu, which is a carryover from the World War I apparel worn by the French army in the early days of World War II. Although the thought of Hitler's head in a pot may have been psychologically and gastronomically appealing, the reality was that France, which had lost close to 1.5 million soldiers in World War I, had no stomach for another war, especially on French soil. Although she had superior manpower, her army went down to humiliating defeat in May 1940. It took the German XIX Panzer Corps only six days to break out of French containment, at which time the French army collapsed.

France, by Pierre Ugrere, Editions Maes, Riviere-Caen, prior to May 1940, value $25-$50.

When war broke out on September 1, 1939, with Germany's invasion of Poland, French artist Maurice Toussaint caught the ill-founded euphoria of the moment by picturing the allies Poland, France, and England in battle dress standing in front of their nation's flags. Little did Toussaint or anyone else realize that less than a year later England would be standing alone against the Nazi war machine. On September 23, Germany announced the end of the Polish campaign with the terse announcement, "The Polish army of a million men had been defeated, captured or routed." On September 30, Poland established a provisional government in Paris. In June 1940 France capitulated, thus leaving England to fight the Nazi menace by herself for more than a year before the United States entered the war.

France, by Maurice Toussaint, Les Editions Militaires Illustrees, 1939.

France, by Paul Barbier, published by P.C. Postcards of Paris, 1939-40, value $25-$50.

French artist Paul Barbier's brilliance as a caricaturist is clearly shown in this card titled "The trio of gangsters" depicting German Propaganda Minister Dr. Joseph Goebbels as a diminutive monkey with a rat tail, Hitler as the Grim Reaper complete with bloody scythe, and the vain, corpulent Hermann Goering, head of the German Luftwaffe (Air Force) as a potbellied, heavily bemedaled gorilla. Barbier's postcards were produced on photographic stock in both English and French by P.C. Postcards of Paris from September 1939 until France capitulated in June 1940.

Other than the gallant performance of the Free French under Charles de Gaulle, France had little to be proud of during the early stages of World War II. After France capitulated in June 1940, de Gaulle and his forces carried on a once proud military tradition. Spurred by shame as well as national pride, a French resistance force known as the Maquis was formed.

De Gaulle appointed Jean Moulin to head the movement and although initially small in numbers, they created considerable havoc through sabotage and supplied some useful information to the Allies. Their numbers grew with each passing year so that by August 1944 they played a major role in liberating Paris from within.

Adri's postcard proudly documents the liberation by drawing on images of the French Revolution. Unfortunately, Moulin was not there to share in the glory. Captured by the Gestapo in June 1943, he was tortured to death. Many secretly - and not so secretly - wished the same for de Gaulle. While undoubtedly patriotic, he was exceedingly prickly, difficult, proud, and capable of seeing anything except subservience as treason. Roosevelt, Churchill, and their generals tended to see little reason why Allied strategy should be predicated on his notions of "La Glorie Francaise," causing de Gaulle to consider them "perfidious," a perception of the English-speaking peoples he held until his death a quarter-century later.

France, by Adri, value $25-$50.

France, by A. Jaegy, Freney, Elbach Dannemarle, value $25-$50.

The sophisticated primitive art of A. Jaegy is greatly sought after by collectors of World War II propaganda postcards. The French artist produced a set of 20 cards, 13 of which are anti-Hitler in nature and illustrated on pages 108 to 113. They are color cards in a red, white, and blue envelope with the message "In spite of you, we remain French." One particular card pictured on page 112 shows the Angel of Death as a gargoyle devil coming to grab two of his own. He hovers smiling over Hitler and Goering on the road to Berlin, which is bordered by countless graves. Popular French propaganda often draws on "high" culture, and bizarre statuary similar to this gargoyle is common in late Gothic cathedrals.

France, by A. Jaegy, Freney, Elbach Dannemarle, value $25-$50.

France, by A. Jaegy, Freney, Elbach Dannemarle, value $25-$50.

France, by A. Jaegy, Freney, Elbach Dannemarle, value $25-$50.

France, by A. Jaegy, Freney, Elbach
Dannemarle, value $25-$50.

France, by A. Jaegy, Freney, Elbach
Dannemarle, value $25-$50.

*France, by A. Jaegy, Freney, Elbach
Dannemarle, value $25-$50.*

*France, by A. Jaegy, Freney, Elbach
Dannemarle, value $25-$50.*

*France, by A. Jaegy, Freney, Elbach
Dannemarle, value $25-$50.*

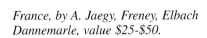

France, by A. Jaegy, Freney, Elbach Dannemarle, value $25-$50.

France, by A. Jaegy, Freney, Elbach Dannemarle, value $25-$50.

France, by A. Jaegy, Freney, Elbach Dannemarle, value $25-$50.

France, by A. Jaegy, Freney, Elbach Dannemarle, value $25-$50.

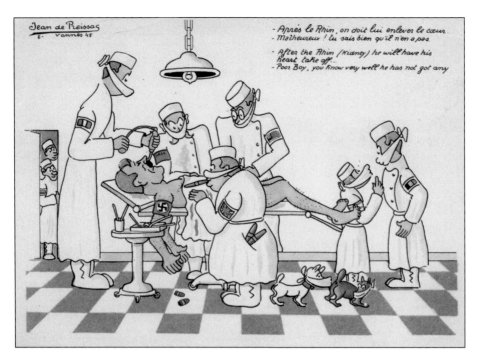

France, by Jean de Preissac, Editions Jipe-Vannes, 1945, value $25-$50.

Allied leaders depicted as surgeons operating on Adolph Hitler is the clever theme of Jean de Preissac's postcard done shortly after France was freed in 1945. The broken English translation reads "After the rhin (kidney) he will have his heart take off...Poor Boy, you know very well he has not got any." The identifiable surgeons are Charles de Gaulle, leader of the Free French, administering the anesthetic; Great Britain's Prime Minister Winston Churchill, with his trademark cigar, to the left of the operating table; and bespectacled United States President Franklin Roosevelt opposite Churchill across the table. With typical patriotic chauvinism, the hospital staff and even the operating room dogs are French. The use of the French word for kidney (rhin) undoubtedly refers to the River Rhine and literally translated can be interpreted, "After crossing the Rhine the Allies will be in the heart of Germany."

Joseph Stalin is the circus ringmaster taming the caged Nazi animals in this clever rendition by French artist Adri. Already mounted on the perches to Stalin's left are Adolph Hitler in the foreground and Vichy French Premier Pierre Laval behind Hitler, with the diminutive Dr. Joseph Goebbels climbing the bars of the enclosure. On the right side of the postcard the grotesquely corpulent Hermann Goering is pleading to do the ringmaster's bidding while Gestapo Chief Heinrich Himmler waits docilely in the background. Although Russia could not have won the war alone, she fought the European land battle by herself from 1941, when Germany invaded, until 1943 when the Allies landed in Italy. Russia's losses in World War II were three times those of Germany. Including civilians who starved, froze, or perished in other irregular ways, Soviet deaths in the second World War are commonly estimated at about 20 million.

France, by Adri, value $50 and up.

Georgi Dimitrov is shown towering over Herman Goering in this photomontage postcard by John Heartfield (Helmut Herzfeld) designed to raise money for the Communist Party in its war against Nazism. Dimitrov, a Bulgarian, was arrested in 1933 as a suspect in the Reichstag fire. During the trial, Dimitrov cleverly succeeded in casting suspicion on the Nazis as the arsonists, causing Minister President Goering, a witness for the state, to totally lose his composure. Although acquitted, Dimitrov was deported to the Soviet Union where he rose to the rank of general in the Russian army. Returning to Bulgaria after the war, he proclaimed the Bulgarian Peoples Republic September 15, 1946, and served as its president until his death.

Heartfield, considered creator and master of the photomontage technique, joined the Communist Party in 1918, producing many fundraising posters and postcards until he was banished by Hitler in 1933. During World War I many Britons of German origin changed their names to avoid linkage to their Germanic roots, most notably the Battenbergs, cousins to the King of England, who became the Mountbattens. Helmut Herzfeld, on the other hand, changed his name to John Heartfield in order to sound British and as an act of defiance against his native Germany. This card was probably published in the United States, but the legend is in both English and German. The English legend reads "In Germany millions of courageous men and women long for anti-Fascist literature. Special means are required to secure transport and replicate this literature. Buying this card you take charge of sponsorship for the belivering (sic) of periodicals to Germany. Price 20c."

France, by John Heartfield (Helmut Herzfeld), value $50 and up.

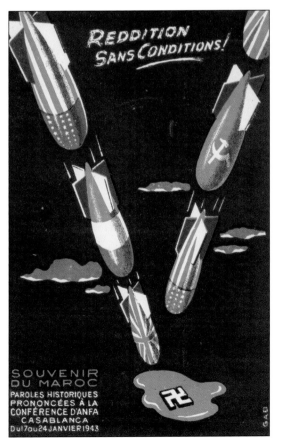

"Peace can come to the world only by the elimination of German and Japanese war power. The elimination of German, Japanese and Italian war power means the Unconditional Surrender of Germany, Italy and Japan." With those words President Franklin D. Roosevelt concluded the conference of the Allied leaders in Casablanca, Morocco, that had been held from January 7-24, 1943. This powerful design by the Moroccan artist Gab shows bombs bearing the flags of England, France, United States, and the Soviet Union raining down in "V for Victory" formation, obliterating the swastika in a pool of blood. Although invited to join Roosevelt and Churchill at Casablanca, Stalin declined because of the critical military situation in Russia but pressed for a second front in Europe. The Casablanca conference also brought together French Generals de Gaulle and Giraud, who at the time were vying to be acknowledged "leader of France." The USSR had no strategic bombers, and the French had no organized military force at all, but the strength of the art is in its symbolic representation of a world alliance united in determination to destroy the Nazi regime. The many disagreements among the Allied powers were subordinated to the common goal of defeating Hitler and the postcard is a memorable souvenir.

Morroco, by Gab, Editions Excelsior Mario Azorin, 1943, value $25-$50.

115

Ten thousand of these 1941 government postcards extolling the virtues of the Greek navy and its brave sailors were issued prior to Greece's surrender in April of that year. King George, who later set up a Greek government in exile in London, is pictured on the printed stamp on this card. The Greek navy continued to make an impact throughout the war. Consisting of 33 ships including submarines, destroyers, and anti-submarine craft manned by 5400 officers and sailors, they served mainly on patrol and convoy duty. Just as important was a Greek force known as "Sea Guerrillas" who operated in the Aegean Sea with a flotilla of some 30 ships they had recaptured from the Italians and Germans.

The gallant Greek defense of its homeland won wide respect and admiration after Italy invaded on October 28, 1940. Benito Mussolini, jealous of the success his Axis partner Adolph Hitler was enjoying, expected a prompt victory for the Italian army. Instead the Italians were humiliated and driven back into Albania from whence the invasion had begun. Hitler came to the rescue, attacking Greece on April 6, six months after Mussolini's aborted invasion; Greece capitulated two weeks later when it became obvious she could not defend herself against both Germany and Italy.

This postcard was produced by the Acropolis Novelty Co. of New York. The verbatim legend on the back says "The immortal Tsolias on October 28, 1940 with the battle cry 'AEPA' (meaning air) frustrated the arrogant plans of an impostor empire to conquer Greece and only yielded when a much greater empire hastened to blot out the disgrace of its defeated ally, April 7 to 27, 1941." This poster-style postcard was featured in an article in *Postcard Collector* magazine (March 1987) where it was termed a "rare linen" which was "printed, published and presumably distributed in the United States for the Greek-American market."

Allied postcard rendered as if Italian, value $50 and up.

The most efficient propaganda is often that which is made to appear as if it is emanating from one side when in reality it is being produced by the other. A perfect example is that extremely rare and colorful series titled "Mussolini is always right." Using one of El Duce's famous slogans, the series uses quotes from the Italian dictator and hurls them back in his face. The card above, for example, shows Mussolini writing on a blackboard "12 x 5 = 22" referring to his quote, "Fascism will last twelve years multiplied by five," while in reality he was driven from power after 22 years. However, he did manage to stay in office ten years longer than Hitler, who was Germany's dictator from 1933 to 1945. The other cards in the set, equally colorful and provocative, are shown on pages 117 to 122 to provide you with a glimpse of the entire series.

Allied postcard rendered as if Italian, value $50 and up.

Allied postcard rendered as if Italian, value $50 and up.

Allied postcard rendered as if Italian, value $50 and up.

Allied postcard rendered as if Italian, value $50 and up.

Allied postcard rendered as if Italian, value $50 and up.

Allied postcard rendered as if Italian, value $50 and up.

Allied postcard rendered as if Italian, value $50 and up.

Allied postcard rendered as if Italian, value $50 and up.

Allied postcard rendered as if Italian, value $50 and up.

*Allied postcard rendered as if Italian,
value $50 and up.*

*Allied postcard rendered as if Italian,
value $50 and up.*

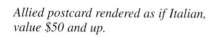

On October 13, 1943, King Victor Emmanual of Italy officially changed sides by declaring war on Germany, after Italy had surrendered on September 3 and after the Allies were fighting the Nazis on Italian soil. In reality, the declaration was little more than a token gesture. Out of 61 Italian divisions, only seven actually fought on the side of the Allies. However, many Italians were glad to escape the Nazi yoke and many had relatives in the United States, making war against Uncle Sam uncomfortable to begin with. Italian artists like Giatila from Florence quickly jumped on the bandwagon and began producing anti-Axis postcards. Borrowing from Shakespeare and the *Hamlet* soliloquy, this postcard is titled "Il Dilemma: Essere o Non Essere" (The Dilemma: to be or not to be). Hitler's dilemma is not knowing which way to turn as he is surrounded by American, British, and Russian forces while he continues to hold a shackled Mussolini clinging tenaciously to a dead bird that had been the black Fascist eagle. Mussolini was dramatically rescued from imprisonment in an Italian mountain resort by German commandos led by Otto Skorzeny in mid September 1943 and ostensibly put back in charge of an Italian empire that no longer existed.

Italy, by Giatila, Florence, P.W.B., Florence, 1943, value $25-$50.

Mexico, published by Second Front Bar, value $25-$50.

Less than six months after the Japanese attack on Pearl Harbor, Mexico joined the Allies on May 27, 1942. Where many Allied governments produced anti-Axis propaganda postcards, Mexico, like the United States, relied on private firms to produce the material. An excellent case in point is this scatological card published by the Second Front Bar titled "Going Down." As the long arm of Uncle Sam is ready to flush Hitler down the toilet while Tojo and Mussolini are laughing, Hitler replies, "Don't laugh at me. You go next." It was not unusual to use war terms such as "Second Front" to name bars and restaurants that catered to soldiers. Although the city where the bar is located is not mentioned, in all probability it was in one of the border towns such as Juarez or Tijuana.

„Wees nou verstandig Adolf en zet 'n advertentie, of ze ergens 'n goeie Führer met toebehooren kunnen gebruiken. Anders komen we binnenkort allemaal op straat te staan!...."

The Netherlands, by Ton Smits, Eindhovensch Dagblad, after the liberation of Holland, value $25-$50.

„Volksgenossen!.... Wir haben noch zwei Tààààànks!.... Es ist noch nichts passiert!....

The Netherlands, by Ton Smits, Eindhovensch Dagblad, after the liberation of Holland, value $25-$50.

Although humorous and somber sound like a contrast in terms, they may best describe the surrealistic art of Ton Smits. His work captured the cold reality of war and made you laugh at the same time. Antonie Gerardus (Ton) Smits was born February 18, 1921, in Veghel, Holland and was only 18 years old when World War II began in September 1939. His formal training was at the Academy of Visual Arts in Den Bosch, the Netherlands. His cartoons were popular worldwide, and he was a frequent contributor to such American weeklies as *The New Yorker* and *Look*. When Eindhoven was liberated by the Allies in June 1944, just after the D-Day invasion, Smits, who was then living there, produced the series of anti-Nazi postcards that are illustrated here.

In one example, Goebbels says to Hitler, "Be clever Adolf, make an announcement in the papers and see if someone wants a good Fuhrer with staff. Otherwise we'll become unemployed." Smits produced a number of comic depictions, many of which were surprisingly mild and demur. In this work Hitler and Goebbels look no more odious than Mutt and Jeff, although one Smits postcard depicts two particularly Neanderthalish Nazis and is simply titled "Ras . . ." - an obvious swipe at the master race.

Uit het Führerhoofdkwartier

„Kijk Adolf,.... das grosze Vaterland?...."

The Netherlands, by Ton Smits, Eindhovensch Dagblad, after the liberation of Holland, value $25-$50.

The Netherlands, by Ton Smits, Eindhovensch Dagblad, after the liberation of Holland, value $25-$50.

Het nieuwe W.A.-uniform....

De bloem van de natie.... Komt dat zien!....

The Netherlands, by Nico Broekman,
May 1945, value $25-$50.

Dutch artist Nico Broekman's skill as a propagandist is
evident by these two postcards. Originally drawn in 1941, a
year after Germany's occupation of Holland, the first shows
the little ways graffiti artists could contribute to the war
effort. Frustrated by the success of the Allies' "V for
victory" campaign, the Nazis adopted it as their own, adding
the words "Germany is victorious on all fronts." They posted
these signs all over the occupied territories. These well-
known German posters were quickly altered by adding a
caricature of Hitler raising his arms in a "V" for surrender
and the "pages" after "front" and HELP above the capitulating Hitler. German news reports in wartime papers were
frequently lies and this clever alteration made unpleasant
truths seem similarly dubious.

The second postcard titled "The Green Police Tyrants"
shows an enraged Nazi thug about to beat up a child who has
drawn a swastika hanging from a gallows and the emblem of
the Dutch royal family underneath. These postcards, for
obvious reasons, were not published openly until the
Netherlands was free, though they did circulate covertly.
The printed message on the left and bottom of the card
reads, "A memory of five distressful years of war, terror and
suppression by Nazis May 1940 - May 1945."

The Netherlands, by Nico Broekman, May 1945, value
$25-$50.

Norway, by Nell Hott, published by Raphael Tuck & Sons, value $25-$50.

Titled "Freedom at Last" by Nell Hott, this postcard was published in England under the auspices of Norway's King Haakon VII to raise money for Norwegian war relief. The postcard shows a Norwegian seaman reunited with his family after escaping his homeland to fight the Nazis. A ship bearing the Norwegian flag is significantly placed in the background. Free Norwegians played their most important role in the Battle of the Atlantic. Always a seafaring people, more than 25,000 Norse sailors worked to bring supplies such as food, oil, airplanes, weapons, and ammunition to Britain and other Allied theaters of war under extremely adverse and dangerous conditions. Norway's four million ton fleet was rebuilt, becoming one of the fastest and most modern in the world. On a daily basis their tankers provided Britain with nearly half of the gasoline and oil supply needed. The thankful British stated that "Norway's tanker fleet was worth more to democracy than 1,000,000 men."

Jerusalem artist Noah Bee produced a series of pro-British postcards and one of his best portrays the centuries old slogan "Britannia Rules the Waves." Throughout her history, sea power enabled Great Britain to survive and to establish a vast empire. A well-fed, healthy-looking but jowly Britannia resembles Brunhilde of Wagnerian opera fame and Bee apparently meant to tweak the Fuehrer's nose, since Hitler greatly admired Wagner. In fact, Britons were far from well-fed, thanks to the success of German submarines that prevented many attempts to bring food from abroad. Britannia's trident contains the skewered heads of Mussolini and Hitler, and the critical success of British forces in the North African desert war remains a staple of her propaganda mythology to the present.

Palestine, by Noah Bee, published by Noah Bee, date of publication unknown, value $25-$50.

Allied for use in Persia, by Kem, published by British Legation, Tehran, Iran, value $50 and up.

Sultan Zahhak of ancient Persian folklore was the personification of evil. So evil that in order for him to remain calm, the two snakes emanating from his neck and shoulders had to be fed the brains of young Persians. The gifted cartoonist Kem, seemingly able to work in any language, resurrects the fable by portraying Hitler as Zahhak; Mussolini and Tojo as the snakes, and Goebbels as the horned devil ready to do his master's bidding. Meanwhile, Kavah, the wise, strong, and brave blacksmith, representing the Allies, informs Zahhak that his evil ways will no longer be tolerated and he will be driven from power. Good does indeed triumph over evil, as the second postcard shows. Kavah, aided by the Allied warriors Roosevelt, Stalin, and Churchill, captures Zahhak (Hitler) and ties him so well "that only the ultimate power can untie him." Note the devil in the person of Josef Goebbels tied to the horse's tail. The other three postcards, part of a five-card set, were produced by the British for use in Iran and continue the story of the fable leading up to Zahhak's - Hitler's - capture.

Allied for use in Persia, by Kem, published by British Legation, Tehran, Iran, value $50 and up.

Allied for use in Persia, by Kem, published by British Legation, Tehran, Iran, value $50 and up.

Allied for use in Persia, by Kem, published by British Legation, Tehran, Iran, value $50 and up.

Allied for use in Persia, by Kem, published by British Legation, Tehran, Iran, value $50 and up.

Poland, by Eligiusz Kanarek, Republic of Poland Exhibition for the New York World's Fair of 1940, value $50 and up.

These poignant postcards are from paintings by Eligiusz Kanarek. "Deportation of Poles from the Annexed Provinces" and "Martyrdom of Polish Children" were available at the Republic of Poland's Exhibition during the 1940 World's Fair in New York, and introduced many Americans to the horrors of the current war for the first time. This group of pathetic refugees walking aimlessly along snow-covered railroad tracks under Nazi guard was among the first of millions left homeless, helpless, and hopeless by the war. Perhaps the most fortunate person in the group is the elderly man sprawled out dead from either a Nazi bullet or exhaustion. He, at least, would suffer no more. Sadly, Kanarek met the same fate as the victim in his drawing: he died in the Warsaw ghetto during the war. On the second postcard, homeless children huddle together for warmth in the ruins of what was once their home in bombed-out Warsaw. The wartime plight of children, mothers, refugees, and the elderly made effective propaganda at this stage of the war, because it seemed apolitical and humanitarian. It is notable that the victims conform to Nazi stereotypes of Aryan racial purity at a time Hitler was proclaiming the Poles to be "subhuman."

Poland, by Eligiusz Kanarek, Republic of Poland Exhibition for the New York World's Fair of 1940, value $50 and up.

Kukryniksy, the most famous and provocative Russian propaganda artist from World War II, is actually three people. This pseudonym, used by three gifted artists whose work spanned three decades, was derived from portions of their names. The "KU" represents Mikhail Kuprinianov and the "KRY" comes from Porfiri*kry*lov, while the first name of Nikolai Sokolov produces "NIKSY." The first three cards illustrated here are examples of their outstanding work.

Titled "Pincer Into Pincers," the first card shows a terrified Hitler entrapped by a Russian Pincer dwarfing his own. The torn paper ripped apart by one of the pincers says, "The Plan for Encircling and Seizing Moscow." The plan failed even though German troops came within 20 miles of Moscow before grinding to a screeching halt on December 5, 1941. On December 6, a massive counter-attack led by Marshall Georgi Zhukov was launched along a 500-mile front around Moscow with Russian troops breaking through on all sides. Thus the encirclers become the encircled. It's one of the war's great turning points and the Kukryniksy captured it brilliantly.

The second Kukryniksy card, produced in 1941, needs no title. It shows a cowering Hitler being protected by Luftwaffe Chief Hermann Goering, whose head has just been blown off by a rain of Russian bombs bearing the Red Soviet star while another Nazi officer suffers the same fate. It's a subtle dig at Goering, who promised Hitler air superiority during the Russian campaign but failed to deliver as the war dragged on. Long-range Russian bomber attacks played havoc with German troops and supplies as Russia, not Germany, took command of the air. Based beyond the range of the Luftwaffe, these bombers played a huge role in Russia's ultimate success.

The fertile imagination of the Kukryniksy is never more evident than in the third classic card produced in 1943, after the tide had turned. Picturing Nazi propaganda minister Dr. Joseph Goebbels inside a phonograph with his head as the stylus and his tongue as the needle, is a stroke of genius. In 1941, when Germany was on the verge of victory, Goebbels was bragging about "Blitzkreig

USSR, by Kukryniksy, published by Russian Propaganda Ministry, value $50 and up.

War" (lightning war) while Hitler proudly listens with chest puffed out. In 1943 a disconsolate Hitler listens with slumped shoulders while an obviously disheveled Goebbels drones on in a completely different tune from 1941. This time his remarks are, "A protracted war is inevitable. We managed to escape from the front and avoid a new Stalingrad." Hitler's refusal to let his troops break out of containment around Stalingrad when there was still time to do so may have cost him the war. More than 90,000 of his finest troops were captured, never to fight for Germany again. Another 200,000 were killed. Note the record playing on the machine is warped. It's little nuances like this that separated the Kukryniksy from other propaganda artists.

The fourth postcard (on page 133) by an unnamed artist shows a smiling Russian soldier in full battle gear with six spent cartridges in his hand proclaiming, "I shoot like this. A German for every round." Behind the soldier are many graves adorned with German helmets. Confidence in the Soviet military rose when they discovered the German soldiers were not invincible and propaganda cards such as this exude that confidence.

The fifth card illustrates the Russian legend that seamen fight like demons when forced into a land battle. In the defense of Leningrad (now St. Petersburg), many sailors were called upon to fight as land troops in order to save the city. This seaman is taking out his revenge on the fallen German. In the background are the spires of two famous St. Petersburg landmarks. This is a New Year's card captioned "A New Year Baltic Salute." Leningrad was under siege from September 15, 1941, until January 27, 1944, when Soviet General Govorov, commander of the Leningrad front, announced that the German blockade had been completely lifted. Close to one million Russian soldiers and civilians were believed to have perished during this period.

USSR, by Kukryniksy, published by
Russian Propaganda Ministry,
1941, value $50 and up.

USSR, by Kukryniksy, published by
Russian Propaganda Ministry,
1943, value $50 and up.

USSR, artist unknown, published by Russian Propaganda Ministry, value $25-$50.

USSR, published by Russian Propaganda Ministry, value $25-$50.

USSR, published by Russian Propaganda Ministry, value $25-$50.

This inspirational postcard features Alexander of Neva, a feudal Russian prince who defeated the Teutons (Germans) centuries before on the River Neva. At the time, much of Russia was occupied by German conquerors. Alexander raised an army of peasants to rise up and overthrow them. The key battle took place on the frozen Neva River. In those days, armies formed a V-shaped phalanx when attacking. Alexander cleverly lured the German knights into an inverted V formed by his own troops closing ranks and then surrounding them. The Teutonic knights were so heavily weighted with armor, many fell through the ice and drowned in the river. As a consequence of his great victory, Prince Alexander became one of Russia's greatest heroes. The top caption reads "The truth is on our side. Struggle until victory." The bottom portion of this card shows a sailor, soldier, and a heavily armed peasant. The great Russian writer Leo Tolstoy once referred to the war of 1812, which ended in the defeat of Napoleon, as the "Peoples War" because many Russian peasants joined in the defense of their homeland and were greatly instrumental in Russia's victory. Under the patriotic graphic appears a quote from Joseph Stalin: "Let the brave images of our great ancestors inspire you in this war." There is a great touch of irony here that needs explaining. When Lenin, Stalin, Trotsky, and other Communist leaders took over control of Russia following the 1917 revolution, one of the first things they did was close the churches and eradicate any vestiges of Russia's past history. To them, everything good in Russia began with the revolution, while anything from the past was bad. However, when Germany attacked Russia in Operation Barbarossa on June 22, 1941, Stalin was smart enough to inspire the masses by reminding them of the past in order to have their full support. Consequently, he reopened churches and resurrected past heroes like Prince Alexander who had become a non-person during nearly 25 years of an often brutal Communist regime.

USSR, published by Russian Propaganda Ministry, value $25-$50.

USSR, published by Russian Propaganda Ministry, value $25-$50.

The Russian bugler, backed by a vast army with heavy artillery and air support, sounds the call. The caption simply reads "Your Motherland Calls YOU." A Russian sailor, heavily armed with a submachine gun and hand grenade for battle on land as well as sea, shouts "Forward! To the West!" The band on his cap reads "Military Sea Fleet" while the Red Star and Hammer and Sickle are prominent in the background.

The final card illustrated is another New Year's card. The sailor is holding an artillery shell marked "For the Motherland." The verse shown below says "Happy New Year. We are beating Germans full speed ahead. I send you my artillery greeting. Combat Baltic Sailor." The messages on these three cards are quite clear. They present members of the Soviet military in a heroic light and are geared to inspire the people.

Some of the postcards pictured here could well have been produced on their famous propaganda trains. According to Anthony Rhodes in his excellent book *Propaganda, The Art of Persuasion: World War II*, "One exclusively Soviet wartime feature was the propaganda railway train. Its compartments were converted into printing presses and portable cinemas and it was staffed with teams of lecturers, actors and artists. They toured the country making speeches and supplying information about the war; they even penetrated into the battle zones, where the train stood in a siding, camouflaged behind the lines." These propaganda trains were the brainstorm of Leon Trotsky, who used them quite successfully during the 1917 revolution to get the Communist message across to the peasants. Most of the Russian population was illiterate at the time, so graphic posters and postcards proved extremely effective. Trotsky, one of the early Communist leaders, was assassinated in Mexico on August 2, 1940. Trotsky became an archenemy of Stalin, who considered him a viable threat to his authority and probably ordered him killed.

USSR, published by Russian Propaganda Ministry, value $25-$50.

I would like to express my thanks to Mikhail A. Shurgalin, Press Counsellor at the Russian Embassy in Washington, D.C., who not only translated the captions on the postcards, but taught me much about Russian World War II propaganda operations as well as Russian history. Mikhail, I am so grateful for your help.

France, prior to June 1940.

"Dire que c'est ça qui veut faire trembler le monde!"

The sport of soccer has as wide a metaphoric appeal in Europe as baseball does in the United States. These three anti-Hitler cards with a soccer theme each come from a different nation. The first, produced in France prior to June 1940, shows a French soldier guarding his goal while a British Tommy admonishes Hitler (depicted as the ball) with the words, "Tell me why it is your wish to make the world tremble (shake up the world)." The second, a Dutch card, shows a Free Dutch soldier booting a Hitler-faced soccer ball in the air with the caption "Well played boys!" It was obviously produced after Holland was liberated in 1944. The third, a Belgian card by A. Fredericks titled "The Winning Goal" shows Harry Truman scoring on a header while Goebbels and Goering have already been knocked to the ground by fellow Allies Churchill and Stalin. It is the only known World War II propaganda postcard featuring Harry Truman, who became President of the United States after the death of Franklin Roosevelt on April 12, 1945. A gloating Hitler, feeling FDR's passing was a good omen, issued an Order of the Day labeling Roosevelt the "Greatest war criminal of all times." Just 17 days later, Hitler was dead by his own hand.

The Netherlands, after 1944.

Belgium, by A. Fredericks, after 1944, value $25-$50.

136

Propaganda Postcards of World War II - The Axis Nations

...a dir le mie virtù basta un sorriso...

DIRIGENTI E MAESTRANZE DELLA
CARLO ERBA S. A. - MILANO
AI CAMERATI COMBATTENTI

Finland, published by Kuvahankinta Co., Helsinki, 1939.

Finland's story is one of the first great tragedies of World War II and one of incomparable heroism. On November 30, 1939, Russia, with its population of 182 million, attacked little Finland with a population of less than four million. Despite these odds, the gallant Finns, using ski troops to perfection, gave Russia more than it could handle for more than three months before finally capitulating on March 11, 1940. Finnish ski troops, wearing all white and known as Bielaja Smert (The White Death), blended in perfectly with the winter snow and seemed to dart out of nowhere, stabbing quickly at Russian formations, cutting them in two, and then surrounding and killing the remnants of the Soviet forces. The entire world sided with Finland, and Great Britain, France, and Poland all promised military aid but the offer came too late and Finland had no choice but to surrender and give Russia the territory she was seeking before the war began.

This classic card produced by the Kuvahankinta Co. in Helsinki is one of the few propaganda postcards made during the brief struggle. A gleeful Satan has lassoed Russian dictator Joseph Stalin and foreign minister Vyacheslav Molotov and is leading them straight to hell. The caption reads "Ha Ha, At last I get what's mine." Both tyrants were accused of unspeakable acts against humanity during their long tenures in power, so the Finnish propagandists anticipated their final reward years before their deaths. Incidentally, Molotov is credited with inventing a gasoline-filled bottle bomb during the Russian revolution that still bears his name as the "Molotov cocktail." Hatred for Russia ran so strong that shortly after Germany attacked Russia on June 22, 1941, Finland joined the Axis powers.

Strong anti-Semitic feeling in Nazi propaganda was apparent long before World War II, as evidenced by this postcard promoting a traveling anti-Jewish exhibition called "The Eternal Jew" at Vienna's Northwest Railroad Station in August 1938. Note the grotesque "Shylockian" appearance the elusive artist has given the central figure with a coin filled outstretched right palm while the left hand holds a whip. A relief map of Germany bearing the Hammer and Sickle of the Bolsheviks is tucked under his arm. Hitler's most despised victims, the Jews, and his most hated political enemies, the Bolsheviks, were frequently depicted as a single threat by the Nazi propaganda machine. Austria was officially reunited with Germany March 13, 1938, and the anti-Jewish campaign began almost immediately. This same traveling exhibition was held in Munich in 1937 and advertised on a postcard with an identical version of the same loathsome image.

This postcard is unusual because it is stamped on the message side of the card with a postmark commemorating the exhibit.

Germany, artist unknown, Vienna, 1938.

"One People, One Country, One Leader" is the headline on this map card celebrating Germany's annexation of Austria, Hitler's birthplace. March 13, 1938, is the official date of the Anschluss in which Austria goes from a free nation to a province of the German Reich. Austrian Chancellor Kurt von Schuschnigg attempted to organize a plebiscite to thwart the Nazi takeover, but to no avail. German troops crossed the border on March 12 just to make certain the annexation would proceed. Hitler had an uncanny ability to take over areas without firing a shot. A year later he grabbed the literal heart of Czechoslovakia known as the Sudetenland, with its large German speaking population, under the guise of protecting them.

Germany, published by Brend'Amour, Simpart & Co., Munich, 1938.

"We Thank Our Fuehrer" is the heading on this card, after Germany officially gained control of the Sudetenland in what was previously part of Czechoslovakia. The date of the takeover was October 1, 1938, but the day of infamy that brought it about was September 30, 1938, when the Munich Peace Accord was signed by Adolph Hitler of Germany, Benito Mussolini of Italy, Edouard Daladier of France, and Neville Chamberlain of Great Britain. Chamberlain was naive enough to label the Munich Accord as a document assuring "Peace in our Time." In reality it was the destruction of Czechoslovakia and the unofficial beginning of World War II. Buoyed by the easy manner in which he got his way, Hitler felt the Allies (England, France, Poland) lacked the intestinal fortitude to stop any future attempts to gain more land. In many respects he was right. Hitler's army occupied the remainder of Czechoslovakia on March 15, 1939, with hardly a whimper from the Allies.

Germany, published by Brend'Amour, Simpart & Co., Munich, 1938.

Germany, by Gottfried Klein, published by NSDAP, Munich, 1939.

Gottfried Klein was another well-known Third Reich artist whose Gothic style art was bold and dramatic. This card titled "Danzig is German" is one of his most famous works. Danzig was a sticking point with most Germans since the end of World War I. At the Treaty of Versailles, despite its heavy German population, Danzig became a free city and a Polish corridor was established, separating Germany from East Prussia. Hitler demanded the return of both. Having seen at Munich that the Allies had no stomach for war, he felt they would cave in once again. The Fuehrer also felt that Poland would accede to his demands and become a German satellite, thus gaining protection from Communist Russia. The Poles refused and at 4:45 a.m. on September 1, 1939, Hitler's Luftwaffe, tanks, and ground troops launched their attack. Just hours after land troops crossed the Polish border, the German battleship *Schleswig-Holstein* opened fire on Danzig. On September 3, Britain and France honored their pact with Poland and declared war on Germany. World War II was underway in earnest. Danzig was indeed once again German but ultimately at a cost of millions of lives and billions of dollars.

Whereas nearly all combatant nations during World War II produced vicious propaganda postcards demeaning their opponents and leaders, German propaganda postcards tended to glorify its Fuehrer, its soldiers, and its citizens, frequently portraying them in heroic roles. Nothing typifies this more than artist Will Tschech's dramatic work titled "Are you not the Standard! Especially at the Front." It shows a German soldier carrying a wounded comrade back to safety and medical attention despite his own wounds. This is probably the most well known propaganda card of the war. Originally in sepia, it was later produced in color. The card was initially issued for the Day of NSDAP (Nazi Party) in General Government, August 13-15, 1943, and posted in Krakau in German-occupied Poland with a special stamp and postmark commemorating the occasion. The only venomous German postcards produced were anti-Semitic in nature (see the Eternal Jew) and these were done before the war. However, German fronts such as the *Swiss Free Press* did indeed resort to defaming the enemy and its leaders although these cards tended to be more humorous than venal.

Nicht **Du** bist der Maßstab! Sondern die **Front!**

Germany, by Will Tschech, published by NSDAP.

Artist Wolf Willrich took great pride in glamorizing German war heroes with his lifelike caricatures of the men. His bold "W" inside "W" and the date represents his easily recognizable signature. Kaptain-leutnant Gunther Prien, commander of the U-47 submarine, was among the most famous and charismatic. Prien first gained attention on October 14, 1939, when he sank the British battleship *Royal Oak*. Prien received a hero's welcome when he returned to Germany and Willrich made him one of his first subjects for adoration on postcards in 1939. July 1940 was considered the "Happy Time" for German U-boats as they sank 38 Allied ships that month alone. But the mortality rate among these undersea heroes was extremely high. Prien met his fate on March 7, 1941, when his U-47 was sunk by the British destroyer *Wolverine*.

Germany, by Wolf Willrich, 1939.

This card titled "The Police in Frontline Duty" shows a member of the German Constabulary Force standing beside a member of the Waffen SS. Printed on the reverse is "Day of the German Police, 1942. Patrol of the Constabulary and the Security Police in the East." The snowy background and the message indicate they were on duty in Russia. By 1942 the Russians were beginning to take back territory lost in the German assault of 1941. When the Germans first occupied Russia, many of the civilians greeted them as liberators because of years of oppression suffered under the Communist regime of Joseph Stalin. However, the Nazi invaders proved to be every bit as brutal as the Communists, causing the citizens to vigorously fight for "Mother Russia." Had Hitler chosen a different tact instead of brutalizing the Russian citizens, he might well have met with success in conquering his adversary.

Germany, 1942.

Italy, by A. Bertiglia, value $25-$50.

Famed Italian artist A. Bertiglia, renowned for his postcards of attractive children as well as military subjects dating to World War I, brilliantly combines the two as these four examples indicate. The first card was produced during the campaign in Ethiopia, showing the natives joyfully worshipping at the feet of their Italian conquerors. This was Benito Mussolini's first attempt to create a new Roman Empire but it was met with stubborn resistance by the poorly equipped Ethiopian army of Emperor Halle Selasie.

The next three cards were all produced in 1941 when things were still going relatively well for the Axis powers. Britain was standing alone against the Axis, as the United States had not yet entered the war. Using cute children to represent Italy, Germany, and Japan, Bertiglia makes them appear much less threatening than they were. In reality, the atrocities they committed both before and after these cards were produced horrified the world. Note the magnificent detail of Bertiglia's work. One card obviously refers to Great Britain's initial defeat in North Africa. It shows a wounded British lion being muzzled by Germany, having his mane sheared by Italy, and his tail about to be cut off by Japan. The forlorn British soldier sits helplessly on the ground after being knocked on the head by the standard bearing the British flag and an umbrella representing Neville Chamberlain, Britain's Prime Minister at the start of World War II, both lying broken nearby.

Another card shows the Axis getting ready to push Great Britain out of Greece and back into the Mediterranean while the wounded dog, depicting Greece, watches in dismay. The Russian bear, drunk on vodka, stumbles around in the background while Uncle Sam watches worriedly, fearful of the Axis might, from across the Atlantic.

The final example shows the Axis goose-stepping through London, which has been destroyed by Axis air power, over the bodies of three terrified British soldiers. At the time these cards were made, that scenario seemed quite possible, but in December 1941, when the United States entered the war, things changed dramatically.

*Italy, by A. Bertiglia,
published by NMM, Milan,
1941, value $25-$50.*

*Italy, by A. Bertiglia,
published by NMM, Milan,
1941, value $25-$50.*

*Italy, by A. Bertiglia,
published by NMM, Milan,
1941, value $25-$50.*

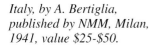

143

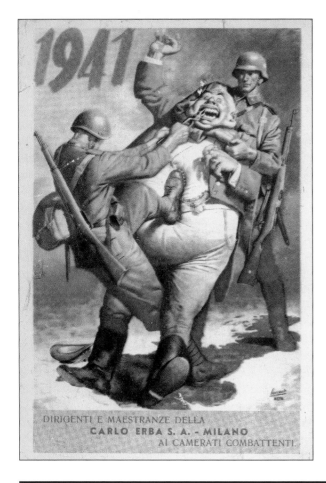

DIRIGENTI E MAESTRANZE DELLA
CARLO ERBA S. A. - MILANO
AI CAMERATI COMBATTENTI.

In 1941 things were not going particularly well for Great Britain and this grotesque Gino Bocassile characterization shows a bloated John Bull having his teeth pulled by an Italian soldier while his Nazi compatriot administers a stranglehold on the beleaguered Briton. Although Bocassile's patriotism is evident in this graphic, in reality, the Italian desert army in Libya was routed by the British until Hitler sent General Erwin Rommel to the North African desert. Launching an attack on March 24, 1941, Rommel drove the British army all the way back to the Libyan port of Tobruk. United States Chief of Staff George Marshall later concluded Germany's over-extension into the desert war to bail out their Italian allies ultimately "became one of the principal factors in Germany's defeat." Though the German commitment to the desert war was never large or important to Hitler, it was very important to Churchill. North Africa was for several years the only place British Empire land forces could hope successfully to fight the Axis, thus greatly magnifying the propaganda significance of this sideshow war.

Italy, by Gino Bocassile, EPOCA-Milano. This was an official postcard published for the Armed Forces, 1941, value $50 and up.

As a Fascist state, Italy's biggest enemy was Bolshevism, invariably depicted on Italian propaganda postcards as a monstrous subhuman. On this postcard entitled "Europe against Anti-Europe," Italy and Germany are portrayed trying to protect the Virgin Mary and Baby Jesus. Note the halos around their heads. It's a subtle attempt by the artist to depict the Communists as anti-Christian as well as subhuman. The monster with the Hammer and Sickle of the Soviet Union at its feet is trying to break down the door of civilized Europe. Geared to create hatred and fear of its primary enemy, Bolshevism, it undoubtedly succeeded because of its directness. Unfortunately, atrocities committed by the Axis were even more heinous than those committed by Soviet forces when they invaded Germany late in the war. Rapes and murders of civilians were rampant on both sides.

Of all the nations in World War II, Italy frequently relied on Christian images to justify its cause, probably because Rome was the cornerstone of the Roman Catholic church. Ironically, during World War I every warring nation used the motto "God is With Us." The message became lost after four years of bitter fighting and millions of deaths and injuries so in World War II it was seldom used.

Italy, published by Cartolina Postale Per Le Forze Armate (official postcard for the armed forces), value $25-$50.

L' EUROPA CONTRO L'ANTIEUROPA

This dramatic piece shows Italian artist Gino Bocassile at his best. With heroic Italian and German soldiers prepared for hand-to-hand combat leading the way, they are followed by the remainder of the Axis forces. Although Germany, Italy, and Japan are the most recognized Axis powers, many other nations fought on their side during the Second World War. Note the various flags in the background. Rumania, Finland, Hungary, Slovakia, Bulgaria, Croatia, and some volunteer units from Spain all fought with the Axis while many divisions from captive nations such as Norway, Belgium, France, Holland, and even Russia were formed. In fact, General Andrei Andreyevitch Vlasov, a publicized Russian war hero during the defense of Moscow, was seized by the Germans, switched sides, and became the highest ranking traitor of World War II. Vlasov recruited an army of over 200,000 from Russian prisoners and fought for Hitler until he was captured by troops commanded by American General George Patton in Czechoslovakia in May 1945. He was turned over to Stalin who had him hanged.

Italy, by Gino Bocassile, value $50 and up.

Italian World War II propaganda postcard art was generally the best executed and most imaginative among the warring nations. Here a smiling Franklin D. Roosevelt gleefully watches American bombs rain down on an Italian city. Note the flames that surge from a hospital building clearly marked with a red cross. Translated from Italian to English the caption reads "A smile is enough to express my virtues." Italian artists frequently depicted Roosevelt as the personification of evil. With his blind, demonic smile and the exploding bombs, Roosevelt is curiously similar to Peter Sellers' portrayal of Dr. Strangelove in Stanley Kubrick's film of that name. Italian-Americans were at the time generally avid Democrats and supporters of President Roosevelt.

Italy, value $50 and up.

145

Gino Bocassile was an ardent Mussolini supporter who produced some of the most graphic and provocative Italian propaganda art of World War II. This classic piece, produced just prior to the Allied invasion of Italy, was designed to strike fear in the hearts of its citizens by depicting the American soldier as a leering, demented black desecrating a church, stealing its treasures, and blaspheming the crucified Savior. Bocassile graphically portrayed the enemy, be it Bolshevism or America, as barbarous subhumans out to destroy his native Italy. He survived World War II, returning to his pre-war career as a highly successful commercial artist until his death in 1952 at the age of 51. Though many Italians had friends and family resident in the United States - not a few of whom served with considerable distinction in the armed forces - propaganda drew on racist stereotypes in all combatant nations.

Italy, by Gino Bocassile, value
$50 and up.

Another fear-provoking postcard by an unknown artist depicts a powerful black - presumably American - soldier ripping the clothes off a struggling Italian woman. It was meant to arouse Italians against the ultimate infamy and dishonor and thus encourage the army to fight: "Defend her! She could be your mother, your wife, your sister, your daughter." Although the Italian army has been justly maligned for performing badly on the field of battle, the defense of their homeland was often heroic, especially when the Nazis offered little choice. It quickly became apparent, however, that few - if any - Allied troops were rape-minded African-Americans costumed in cowboy hats, so this kind of propaganda probably did not help Fascist credibility a great deal.

Italy, artist unknown, official postcard
for use by Italian armed forces, value
$50 and up.

difendila!

POTREBBE ESSERE TUA MADRE
TUA MOGLIE, TUA SORELLA, TUA FIGLIA

Many of the warring nations used national heroes from the past to inspire their soldiers and people to greater heights. In 1944, when things were going badly for the Italians, they called upon "The Spirit of Goffredo Mameli" to "Defend the Republic." Mameli was a patriot who fought and died for Guiseppe Garibaldi's Red Shirt army that defeated the Austrian rulers of Italy in 1848. Borrowing Garibaldi's idea, Mussolini dressed his Fascist supporters in black shirts, while Hitler copied the idea ten years later, choosing brown as his shirt color of choice. The Italians hoped just the mention of Mameli's name would do the same thing for the Italian army against the Allies in 1944. Note how the unnamed artist cleverly merges Mameli in front of an Italian army comprised half of soldiers from 1848 and half from the Italian army of 1944. This came out as both a poster and postcard and ranks among the more beautiful pieces of propaganda art produced during the war.

The Allies first landed on Italian soil on June 11, 1943, when Pantelleria, one of the outer islands, surrendered without a fight. Operation Husky, the invasion of Sicily, began on July 10 and proved to be a lot tougher for the Allied forces, who needed six weeks to quell the opposition. Even then, 49,000 Germans and 62,000 Italians were evacuated across the Messina Strait to the mainland to fight another day. Fighting was still going on in parts of Italy when the war ended in 1945, so perhaps the Mameli postcards were effective.

Italy, official armed forces postcard, 1944.

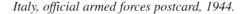

Song postcards have always been popular, but particularly so during wars. World War I saw a plethora of them from all nations featuring patriotic themes intended to boost morale. World War II continued the trend with Germany and Japan particularly active in publishing song postcards. In fact, as early as 1931, *The Horst Wessel* song was printed on dozens of different Nazi postcards glorifying Wessel, an SA member killed in a street brawl with Communists on February 23, 1930. The song written by Wessel was actually titled "Die Fahne Hoch" (The Flag is High) and extolled the virtues of the Nazis.

This Japanese song postcard features the "Love My Country March" which translated says, "We will fight for our country, Our dreams will flower (come true)." The unidentified artist, who signed with a block "S," shows soldiers bearing the Axis flags marching in step together. Intended primarily to evoke patriotism and national pride among civilians, the card says "Citizens Spirit Government March. The Government Information Service recommends this song." There was almost no dissent in Japan during the war and this song would be extremely well received.

Japan, value $25-$50.

This determined - and bulky - Japanese soldier shown by artist Saburo Miyamoto trampling on American and British flags says, "We will not stop shooting." Published by the Japanese Ministry of the Army in celebration of its 38th anniversary, the image typified the resolve to fight to the last man, as they did on occasion, particularly in the early years of the war. The soldier in this postcard is clearly well-fed, well-armed, and, from the size of his backpack, well-provisioned. He is also remarkably Western, looking more like an Asian GI Joe than the grotesque buck-toothed and near-sighted Japanese created by American cartoonists.

Japan, by Saburo Miyamoto, published by Japanese Ministry of the Army, value $50 and up.

Japan, by Kenji Yoshioka, value $25-$50.

December 7, 1941, was a day of infamy in the United States; in Japan it was a time for glorious celebration. At 7:55 a.m. Hawaiian time, 423 Japanese planes attacked Pearl Harbor and surrounding military installations, inflicting heavy damage. Led by Commander Fuchida, the first wave consisted of 40 torpedo bombers, 51 dive bombers, 50 high level bombers, and 43 fighters, with a second wave of similar strength following a short time later. The attack was planned by Admiral Isoroku Yamamoto and launched from six aircraft carriers, *Akagi, Kaga, Hiryu Soryu, Zuikaku*, and *Shokaku*, and was a complete tactical and strategic surprise.

Although the United States lost two battleships, the *Arizona* and *Oklahoma*, in the attack and three others, *California, Nevada,* and *West Virginia* were badly damaged, three aircraft carriers were at sea and escaped the carnage. Three United States cruisers and three destroyers were also sunk and 188 American planes were destroyed, mostly on the ground, along with 2,400 men killed and 1,200 wounded. The Japanese lost only 29 planes. So, from their point of view, the attack was a monumental success. Artist Kenji Yoshioka records the event on a propaganda postcard simply titled "Attacking Pearl Harbor, Hawaii." The brief description spoke volumes. Ironically, Admiral Yamamoto, architect for the attack who spent much pre-war time in the United States and feared American production would ultimately doom Japan in a protracted war, proved correct. Yamamoto himself was killed April 18, 1943, when his plane was shot down over Bougainville.

Japanese postcard artists such as Saburo Miyamoto took great pride in celebrating all of their nation's military victories during World War II, most of which came before 1943. None was more glorious than their victory over the British at Singapore. On December 8, 1941, the Japanese 25th Army, under the command of General Tomoyuki Yamashita, landed in Malaya and rapidly advanced toward the key city and port of Singapore. British Empire forces consisting of troops from Australia and India, as well as Great Britain, were continually pushed back until January 25, 1942, when Field Marshall Sir Archibald Wavell, in charge of Far East operations, ordered General Sir Arthur Percival to retreat to the vaunted island citadel of Singapore itself.

Singapore was considered an impregnable fortress but all its guns and fortifications pointed toward the sea. Wisely, General Yamashita attacked through the jungles of Malaysia and on February 15, the battle was over. General Yamashita accepted the surrender of General Percival and over 70,000 of his men. His remarks to General Percival at the surrender were terse and cold: "All I want to know from you is yes or no." It was the greatest military disaster in British history and certainly ranks among the crowning achievements for Japan in World War II.

Propaganda postcards of this type were available to Japanese troops in order to instill pride in them as well as the people at home. The same image on this postcard showing a British soldier bearing the white surrender flag was captured on newsreels and still photographs shown around the world. Incidentally, General Yamashita, the hero of Singapore who later commanded Japanese forces in the Philippines, was executed as a war criminal in December 1945 for his part in the Bataan Death March in 1942.

Japan, by Saburo Miyamoto, value $25-$50.

One of Japan's more successful propaganda ploys of World War II was the establishment of the "Greater East Asia Co-Prosperity Sphere." This was proposed to link all of Asia together economically, with Japan as the center. It was intended to undermine mainly American but also British, French, and Dutch colonial control over much of East Asia. In other words, "Asia for the Asians." On its propaganda postcards, Japanese soldiers were depicted as benevolent friends, kind to children and adored in return. Folksy postcards like this, issued with rations, served two purposes. They were intended to allow the busy soldier to quickly communicate with loved ones back home simply by drawing or pasting his facial picture on the card as well as pointing out the success of the Co-Prosperity Sphere.

In the beginning many natives were pleased to see the Japanese arrive after their forces quickly took control of the Philippines, Malaya, Indochina, and the Dutch East Indies, to mention only a few. But the brutality of their military reign proved even harsher than the colonial empires it had replaced. The Co-Prosperity Sphere did serve one useful purpose: It enabled most of the countries in East Asia to gain total independence following the war.

These two cards are among the better examples of how the Japanese promoted the Co-Prosperity Sphere. The first says, "Please draw in the face" and shows a Japanese soldier holding two children from newly conquered islands while two more cling to his trousers in a show of great affection. Among the captured areas at this time, in the early 1940s, were Burma, French Indochina (Vietnam), the Dutch East Indies (Indonesia), Malaya, and Singapore. Therefore, this card could be used in any of those countries.

The second card titled "Japan is Friendly" shows a Japanese soldier shaking hands with a native and saying, "The Japanese Army will be rebuilding the country." The local resident replies, "Thank You. We are going to help," while the young boy

Japan, value $25-$50.

approaching with a melon says, "Please eat these." While the Co-Prosperity Sphere was well received at first, the well-documented brutality of the Japanese occupiers, added to the false promises of economic improvements, doomed it to failure. Late in the war, when the tide of victory had turned against Japan, Allied propaganda leaflets ridiculed the idea, referring to it as the "Co-Poverty Sphere."

Japan, value $25-$50.

149

Propaganda Postcards of World War II - The Neutral Nations

Brenden Bracken, a close friend of Winston Churchill, became Minister of Information (MOI) in July 1941. He was the fourth to hold the post since 1939 and finally brought stability and direction to the MOI. In November 1941, Bracken decreed that British propaganda should center on such well-established themes as British military superiority while attacking Nazi policy and propaganda as fraudulent. These two postcards published by the MOI for distribution in neutral Portugal combined these themes beautifully. Using direct quotations from German radio and press accounts of the war, a small portion of each postcard gives the specific date of the German boast with the rest of the card devoted to the British response.

On the first postcard, the German's boast of August 22, 1939, is "No enemy however strong will be able to carry the war into Germany in the air." In the larger panel there are two inscriptions. The larger reads "June-July 1941 R.A.F. Bomb Germany 113 times in 33 days," while under the cartoon a line reads "Up to July 20th, 1941, the R.A.F. bombed Germany alone 1,800 times."

On the second card, a German boast of September 5, 1941, states "The effect of U-boat warfare is becoming more deadly." The rebuttal has a German U-boat commander confessing on September 4, 1941, "British convoys are greatly strengthened, and British planes and war ships chase German submarines away." At the bottom of the postcard is the question "Who should know best?"

These postcards were widely distributed in Portugal where 80% of the population sided with Great Britain. These cards were also published in English for home consumption; but are most commonly found today in Portuguese.

British, published in Portugal by the British Ministry of Information, value $25-$50.

British, published in Portugal by the British Ministry of Information, value $25-$50.

Portugal, by Phillip Zec, 1941.

Just when Hitler felt he had pounded the last nail in France's coffin, the corpse's hand forces the lid open far enough to allow it to paint the "V for Victory" sign on the wall. This cartoon by Phillip Zec appeared in the *London Daily Mirror* on July 17, 1941, with the caption "Very Much Alive." (The unfortunate allusions to Count Dracula are certainly unintentional.) It was reproduced as a postcard in Portugal, which although neutral during World War II, was England's oldest ally. Propagandists on both sides in Portugal issued postcards trying to sway public opinion in their favor and many of them are intriguing. Zec appeared clairvoyant when only two days after this cartoon first appeared, the BBC broadcast the existence of resistance forces in Hitler's Festung Europa. In France they were known as the Maquis; while militarily insignificant and routinely infiltrated by the Nazis, the Resistance quickly became a staple of popular mythology. The "V for Victory" itself originated with Belgian broadcaster Victor de Lavaleye and, like his ubiquitous cigar, it became a Churchill trademark. In utter frustration, the Germans adopted the sign themselves, claiming it stood for Viktoria (German Victory). They were doubtless infuriated by the cant British association of the Morse code for "V" (...-) and the first four notes of Beethoven's Fifth Symphony, which the BBC reinforced with great frequency in both domestic and overseas broadcasts.

„ — Come on, Franklin!"

Portugal, published by Freiheitsverlag Schweiz, *a German front.*

Although it remained neutral during World War II, Portugal was a hotbed for propaganda postcards. Despite a leaning toward England, its oldest ally, there was plenty of pro-German sentiment throughout the country. Another neutral nation, Switzerland, stayed out of the conflict but had many German sympathizers among its people. Throughout the war *Frelheitsverlag Schweiz* (Swiss Free Press) churned out many anti-Allies cards printed in black on poor quality, cream-colored board for use in Portugal. One of the most chilling shows Death inviting President Roosevelt to bring America into the war. It is somehow made all the more effective with the simple caption "Come on, Franklin!" Surrounded by the masts of sunken British ships, Death beckons America to the same fate, flashing a seductive skull-leer.

The Germans became so cocky over their early successes they felt America would offer no challenge, particularly against the German submarines that raised havoc with Allied shipping. In fact, during the first seven months of 1942, after America entered the war, 681 Allied ships were sunk by German U-boats. Such elementary precautions as an east coast blackout and the publication of false shipping schedules, together with protected convoys and advances in undersea detection, diminished the threat, which was ended after ULTRA succeeded in breaking the U-boat ciphers on a regular basis.

This postcard was ostensibly published by the *Frelheitsverlag Schweiz*, but in reality was a product of the Nazi propaganda machine. Gordon Gilkey, Curator Emeritus of the Portland (Oregon) Art Museum, who, during World War II headed the Joint Chiefs of Staff Study of Nazi Psychological Warfare, considers this an excellent example of German black propaganda. On examining a group of *Frelheitsverlag Schweiz* postcards, Gilkey commented, "I am 98% certain that the so-called *Swiss Free Press* was not free and not Swiss...anymore than the German American Bond was American."

O SUICÍDIO DO LEÃO BRITÂNICO

Portugal, published by Freihtsverlag Schweis, *a Nazi front.*

For the most part British propaganda worked extremely well in neutral Portugal and the vast majority of the people were pro-British and pro-Allies. This was not true, however, of Britain's ally Russia, as the Communist regime of Joseph Stalin was both feared and not trusted. The fear and loathing of Stalin by the Portuguese government was so apparent that his face was not even shown in newspapers and newsreels in Portugal until the final year of the war. The Nazi-controlled *Swiss Free Press* was quick to take advantage of this situation by producing postcards such as this example: "The Suicide of the British Lion," showing a bewildered British lion committing suicide with the Hammer and Sickle symbol of Soviet Russia. Since the autocratic regime of Antonio Salazar bred discontent in Portugal, particularly among the workers, the government felt uneasy about Russia assuming a dominant position in the world affairs. The German ploy of drawing attention to the British-Russian alliance with cartoons such as this was effective not only with the Portuguese but with the British themselves. Churchill, in fact, suggested to Roosevelt a possible late war attack on the Russians who were weakened by four years of bitter fighting with Germany.

The disaster at Dieppe on the coast of France was one of the most embarrassing losses the Allies suffered during World War II. On August 19, 1942, a force of approximately 6,000 mostly Canadian troops augmented by British Commandos and American Rangers made a nine-hour landing. More than half were killed, wounded, or captured and the remainder went scurrying home to England. The Dieppe Raid proved for the moment that Germany's "Fortress Europe" could not be breached and nearly two years elapsed before the Allies finally succeeded with the D-Day invasion of Normandy. Meanwhile, the debacle at Dieppe was chronicled in Portuguese by a Nazi front organization calling itself the *Swiss Free Press* in this postcard showing Churchill and Roosevelt being kicked out, while Churchill tearfully exclaims, "At what port can we land our soldiers now?"

O Porteiro - aqui não se brinca aos soldados!!!...

Portugal, published by Freiheitsverlag Schweis, *a Nazi front.*

154

Much of the Nationalist propaganda centered on the Marxist makeup of the Republican government; this anti-Marxist edition produced in Seville shows a beleaguered Prime Minister Manuel Azana being compared to Roman Emperor Nero by fiddling while Madrid burns during the uprising (July 17-20, 1936) throughout Spain and Morocco. The Azana government fell shortly afterwards and turmoil raged throughout the country for three more years.

Spain, published by Ikon-Plastica de Arte, San Sebastian, value $25-$50.

On July 18, 1936, five days after Nationalist leader Calvo Sotelo was murdered by Spanish government security agents, army generals and their troops staged a revolt against the leftist Republican government. This was the beginning of the Spanish Civil War that lasted three years, marked by horrible atrocities on both sides. The rebellion would never have succeeded had it not been for the arrival of General Francisco Franco and his well-trained African Foreign Legion from Morocco, airlifted to southern Spain by planes from Germany and Italy. Franco had convinced Hitler and Mussolini that his cause was a worthy one, since he was fighting against Russian Bolshevism as they were. The battle lines were quickly drawn as Russia and leftists the world over joined the Republicans while Hitler and Mussolini sent troops and equipment to Franco's Nationalists that ultimately turned the tide in Franco's favor. Germany's Condor Legion of crack ground troops and 47,000 troops from Italy comprised 40% of the Nationalist forces. Even more important, 100 German planes commanded by World War II ace General Adolf Galland gave the Nationalists complete air superiority. In many respects, the Spanish Civil War, with the bombing and other tactics developed there, was a training ground for World War II.

This Republican postcard showing a Russian soldier, Marianne of France, John Bull of Great Britain, and Uncle Sam of the United States, is basically a plea for France, Britain, and the United States to join Russia and Spain in the fight against the Nationalists. Although all of these countries provided volunteer forces such as the Lincoln Brigade from the United States, the governments themselves never got involved. In three languages the card says, "The union of the democratic nations will end war forever. Catalunya is continuing to bend all her efforts to the end that the year 1938 will bring both peace and victory to Spain." Franco's forces won the war with the fall of Madrid on March 27, 1939. The Generalisimo ruled Spain until his death in 1975. Despite pleas by both Hitler and Mussolini, who were largely responsible for his success, Franco kept Spain neutral during World War II. Consistently frustrated by Franco's refusal to join the Axis in their war against the Allies, Hitler is reported to have said, "I'd rather undergo a root canal (dental surgery) without Novocain than try to reason with Franco."

Spain, by L.C.T., published by D.A.G., mailed Nov. 17, 1938, value $50 and up.

Spain, published by Minister of Propaganda, mailed May 1937, value $50 and up.

War "breeds strange boat fellows" is the theme depicted on this Spanish Republican propaganda postcard, probably the most famous issued during the Spanish Civil War. It shows the heavily armed Nationalist Burgos Junta, consisting of the improbable alliance of Bishop, General, Nazi Capitalist, and Moor sailing from Lisbon with a gallows-mast bearing Franco's slogan "Spain Arise," while the noose tightens around Spain's neck. The art owes much to Juan Gris and Pablo Picasso, both of whom were Spanish by birth, French by residence, and anti-Fascist by conviction.

About the Author

Ron Menchine was only 11 years old on August 15, 1945, when Japan surrendered unconditionally to bring World War II to a close, but he has vivid memories of those war years. His late father, Judge W. Albert Menchine, spent three years in the Unites States Army Counter Intelligence Corps in Australia, New Guinea, the Philippines, and Korea. His frequent letters home spawned an interest in World War II that remains to this day.

A 1956 graduate of the University of Maryland in Radio-TV and Journalism, Menchine has written three books on baseball history and this one on World War II propaganda postcards. From 1956 through 1958 Menchine was a United States Army Broadcast Specialist, Office, Chief of Information, Military District of Washington (MDW), serving under Col. George Creel, whose father George, Sr. headed the Committee on Public Information in World War I. Col. Creel's father was one of the first to recognize the value of posters and their art that could be converted into postcards, as some of the better ones were. He stated, "I had the conviction that the poster must play a great part in the fight for public opinion." The postcard illustrated here, by an anonymous publisher, is an authentic propaganda card that left space for a soldier, sailor, or marine to insert his picture and become an instant hero in the fight against the Axis. Note the terrified looks on the faces of Hitler, Mussolini, and Tojo as they read the headlines in the bogus newspaper, *The Daily Journal*. Using artistic license, Menchine has substituted his own face, guaranteed to strike even more fear in the hearts and minds of the Axis leaders. World War II propaganda postcards are great fun, most are humorous, some are provocative and horrific, many are scatological and all are fascinating.

A baseball memorabilia and military propaganda collector for more than half a century, Menchine's primary interest is in postcards. From a collection of postcards numbering in the thousands, he has selected 300 of the best dealing with the propaganda aspects of the war, more than half being in color. Cards from 25 different nations are featured, lending an international flavor to the book.

Semi-retired and living in Long Green, Maryland, Menchine was the last radio voice of the Washington Senators baseball team. In addition to Major League Baseball, he has broadcast play-by-play football, basketball, boxing, and soccer for the ABC, CBS, Mutual, and NBC radio networks and had principle roles in the motion pictures *All The President's Men* and *The Seduction of Joe Tynan*. He is the author of *Tuff Stuff's Baseball Postcard Collection* and is presently working on a fifth book, *Presidential Campaign Postcards*, which he will co-author with political historian Leon Rowe. Menchine welcomes inquiries on all his books at P.O. Box 1, Long Green, MD 21092.

Bibliography

Boehm, Edwards, *Behind Enemy Lines, World War II Allied/Axis Propaganda*, Secaucus, NJ: The Wellfleet Press, 1989.

Carr, Raymond, *The Spanish Civil War, A History in Pictures*, New York: W.W. Norton & Co., 1986.

Douglas, Roy, *The World War 1939-1945, The Cartoonists Vision*, London, Routledge, 1990.

Editors of *Yank, The Best from Yank, the Army Weekly*, New York: E.P. Dutton & Co., Inc., 1945.

Grunberger, Richard, *The 12-Year Reich*, New York: Holt, Rinehart & Winston, 1971.

Holt, Tonie & Valmai, *I'll Be Seeing You, Picture Postcards of World War II*, Ashbourne, Derbyshire, England: Moreland Publishing Co., Ltd., 1986.

Lynx, F.F., *The Pen Is Mightier*, London: Lindsay Drummond Ltd., 1946.

Miller, Frances Treveleyan, *History of World War II*, Philadelphia: Universal Look & Bible House, 1945.

Rawls, Walton, *Wake Up America, World War I and the American Poster*, New York: Abbeville Press Publishers, 1988.

Rhodes, Anthony, *Propaganda, The Art of Persuasion World War II*, New York: Chelsea House Publishers, 1976.

Rutherford, Ward, *Hitler's Propaganda Machine*, London: Bison Books Ltd., 1978.

Sommerville, Donald, *World War II, Day by Day*, Greenwich, Connecticut: Brompton Books Corp., 1989.

Stallings, Laurence, *The First World War, A Photographic History*, New York: Simon and Schuster, 1933.

Sulzberger, C.L., *The American Heritage Picture History of World War II*, American Heritage Publishing Co., Inc., 1966.

Szyk, Arthur, *The New Order*, New York: G.P. Putnam's Sons, 1941.

Think *Magazine's Diary of United States Participation in World War II*, New York: International Business Machines Corp., 1950.

Zeman, Zbynak, *Selling the War, Art and Propaganda in World War II*, London: Orbis Publishing Ltd., 1978.

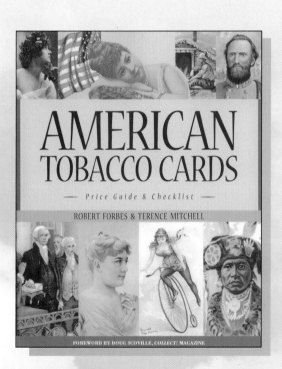

BOOKS TO HELP CONSTRUCT
A GREAT BATTLE PLAN FOR BUILDING
YOUR MILITARY COLLECTION

World War II Homefront Collectibles

Price & Identification Guide

by Martin Jacobs

The war-related keepsakes and novelties produced from 1941-1945, known today as "homefront" collectibles, are highly desired memorabilia that reflect the unifying efforts of a nation. Jewelry, postcards, movie posters, matchbooks, banks, statues, toys, games, trading cards, books, magazines and anti-axis memorabilia - it's all here, profusely illustrated with more than 600 photos and more than 2,000 accurate and detailed price listings.

Softcover • 8-1/2 x 11 • 192 pages
600 color photos • 60+ b&w photos
WWCO • $22.95

Collector's Guide to British Army Campaign Medals

by Robert W.D. Ball

Here's a complete reference that will appeal to collectors of militaria, or anyone interested in world or military history. Fascinating glimpses of the British Empire unfold in this detailed study of medals awarded to British Army troops over more than two centuries. Covers military battles and campaigns waged from 1791 through the Gulf War.

Hardcover • 8-1/2 x 11 • 160 pages
100 b&w photos • 200 color photos
AT5641 • $29.95

American Military Collectibles Price Guide

by Ron Manion

From the Civil War to the Gulf War, this first-of-its-kind price guide to American Military collectibles covers it all. Over 5,800 items from insignia and uniforms to edged weapons and medals are described in detail and accurately priced.

Softcover • 6 x 9 • 288 pages
330 b&w photos
AT5471 • $16.95

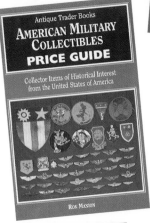

German Military Collectibles Price Guide

by Ron Manion

This comprehensive reference guide covers a full range of militaria from the Kaiser to Nazi Germany. It prices daggers, swords, side arms, medals and all insignia from the German military over the past 150 years.

Softcover • 6 x 9 • 316 pages
500 b&w photos
AT5447 • $16.95

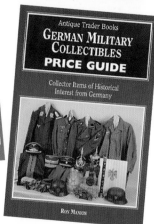

Japanese & Other Foreign Military Collectibles Price Guide

by Ron Manion

Thousands of entries for a wide range of militaria associated with the nations of the world. Includes medals, uniforms and insignia from Japan, Vietnam, Italy, Russia, and more. Detailed descriptions with current prices.

Softcover • 6 x 9 • 248 pages
450 b&w photos
AT5439 • $16.95

Military Small Arms of the 20th Century

7th Edition

by Ian V. Hogg and John Weeks

This is the complete and ultimate small arms reference by Ian Hogg, international military arms authority. Now expanded and updated to include every arm in service from 1900 to 2000; complete with specifications, history and insightful commentary on performance and effectiveness. There is no comparable book.

Softcover • 8-1/2 x 11 • 416 pages
800+ b&w photos
MSA7 • $24.95

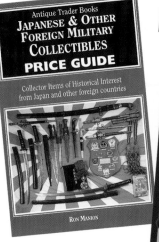